Collins
AP

Lectures

Learn listening and note-taking skills

Fiona Aish and Jo Tomlinson

Academic Skills Series

Collins

HarperCollins Publishers
77-85 Fulham Palace Road
Hammersmith
London W6 8JB

First edition 2013

Reprint 10 9 8 7 6 5 4 3 2 1 0

ISBN 978-0-00-750712-2

Collins® is a registered trademark of HarperCollins
Publishers Limited

www.collinselt.com

A catalogue record for this book is available from the
British Library

Typeset in India by Aptara

Printed in China by South China Printing Co. Ltd

€ You can trust Collins COBUILD

The 4.5-billion-word Collins Corpus is the world's largest
database of the English language. It is updated every
month and has been at the heart of Collins COBUILD
publishing for over 20 years. All definitions provided in
the glossary boxes in this book have been taken from the
Collins COBUILD Advanced Dictionary.

The Publisher and author wish to thank the following
rights holders for the use of copyright material:

Extract from *Pursuit of Innovation lecture* by Ammon
Salter http://wwwf.imperial.ac.uk/imedia/content/
view/1414/the-pursuit-of-innovation--10-march-2011/
reproduced by permission of Ammon Salter

Figure from Thurman, Harold V.; Trujillo, Alan P.,
Essentials of Oceanography, 7th Edition © 2002, p.240.
Reprinted by permission of Pearson Education, Inc.,
Upper Saddle river, NJ

Photograph of Howard Gardener p141: ©2000 Getty
Images

If any copyright holders have been omitted, please contact
the Publisher who will make the necessary arrangements
at the first opportunity.

About the authors

Fiona Aish has taught, designed and managed English for Academic Purposes courses at several universities and language schools in the UK. Nowadays she works with postgraduate students on developing their academic skills and dissertation writing.

Jo Tomlinson has worked at a number of universities and language schools in the UK, teaching both general and academic English. She currently delivers workshops and tutorials for postgraduate students on academic skills and dissertation development.

Jo and Fiona are now directors of Target English Ltd, a company specialising in teaching English for Academic Purposes and English for exams. They have co-authored three books in the Collins English for Exams Series: *Listening for IELTS, Grammar for IELTS* and *Get Ready for IELTS: Writing*.

Acknowledgements

We would like to thank all our students and fellow teachers, in particular Kate, Elisha, Inghar, Omar and Diego, who have been a great source of information for the material in this book. Also, our thanks go to the team at Collins ELT for their support and guidance.

We would like to dedicate the book to Andy Heywood and Margaret Carvell.

HarperCollins and the authors would like to thank the following contributors for kindly allowing us to record and use their lectures to provide authentic listening practice: Dr Suzanne Hagan & Dr Uma Shahani, Glasgow Caledonian University; Professor Bruce D. Malamud, King's College London; Dr Joanna Royle, The University of Glasgow; Professor Ammon Salter, Imperial College Business School; Jenny Siklos, Madison English as a Second Language School.

Contents

- evaluating arguments and views in a lecture
- applying critical thinking
- connected speech and the 'schwa'
- rhetorical questions

- different note-taking systems
- taking notes quickly
- relative clauses
- rising and falling intonation

- the importance of notes for assessments
- rewriting notes
- organizing paper and electronic notes
- keeping notes accurate
- using context to help with understanding

- listening in tutorials
- listening in seminars
- different university systems
- pronunciation revision
- polite language

- know your strengths and weaknesses
- making an improvement plan
- speaker 'mistakes'
- pronunciation review

Introduction

Collins Academic Skills Series: Lectures will give you the skills you need to listen to and understand lectures.

Designed to be used on a self-study basis to support English for Academic Purposes or study skills courses, it is intended for students on pre-sessional or Foundation courses as well as for first year undergraduate students. It will also be useful for more experienced students who want to improve their library-based research skills.

The book has ten chapters covering the key skills for listening to lectures and taking notes. There are also five authentic lectures to give you realistic practice. You will learn how to:

- prepare for a lecture
- recognise different lecture structures
- follow the key points of a lecture
- understand lecturers' accents and speaking styles
- take notes and use them for assessments
- evaluate your listening ability

At the back of the book there is:

- a glossary of key terms
- a comprehensive answer key

Chapter structure

Each chapter includes:

- Aims – These set out the skills covered in the chapter.
- A self-evaluation quiz – By doing this you are able identify what you already know on the subject of the chapter and what you need to learn.
- Information on academic expectations and guidelines on how to develop academic skills – These sections will help you understand university practices and expectations so you know what is required.
- Practical exercises – These help you to develop the skills to succeed at university. You can check your answers at the back of the book.
- Tips – Key points are highlighted for easy reference and provide useful revision summaries for the busy student.
- Glossary – Difficult words are glossed in boxes next to where the text appears in the chapter. There is also a comprehensive glossary at the back of the book.
- Remember sections – This is a summary of key points for revision and easy reference.

Authentic lectures

The book uses examples of authentic lectures in different academic subjects in the authentic lectures chapters. The authentic lectures together with the accompanying exercises provide supported practice of the academic listening skills needed to understand lectures at university.

Glossary boxes `POWERED BY COBUILD`

Where we feel that a word or phrase is difficult to understand, we have glossed this word/ phrase. All definitions provided in the glossary boxes have been taken from the *COBUILD Advanced Dictionary*. At the end of the book there is a full alphabetical list of the most difficult words from the book for your reference.

Using *Lectures*

You can either work through the chapters from Chapter 1 to Chapter 10 or you can choose the chapters and topics that are most useful to you. The Contents page will help in your selection.

Study tips

- Each chapter will take between three and four hours depending on how many times you listen to the audio scripts. Take regular breaks and do not try to study for too long. Thirty to sixty minutes is a sensible study period.
- Regular study is better than occasional intensive study.
- Read the chapter through first to get an overview without doing any exercises. This will help you see what you want to focus on.
- Try the exercises before checking the Answer key. Be an active learner.
- After doing the listening exercises in the book, you may want to do them again to try to understand more of the content.
- All university departments are different. Use the information in the book as a guide to investigating your own university department.
- Write questions you can ask to find out how your department delivers lectures, seminars and tutorials.
- There is no one correct way of listening to lectures and taking notes. Use your experience of doing the exercises to learn what works best for you. Adapt the suggestions in this book to suit your learning style and context.
- Learning to listen to lectures and take notes is an on-going process, which means you need to practise the same skills many times. Revise regularly.

Other titles

Also available in the *Collins Academic Skills Series: Writing, Research, Numbers, Presenting,* and *Group Work*.

1 | The purpose of lectures

Aims ✓ recognize different types of listening
✓ understand what a lecture is
✓ know what is expected from you

✓ recognize possible problems in lectures
✓ understand the importance of attending lectures

Quiz
Self-evaluation

Read the statements below and circle the answers that are true for you.

1	I know who speaks in a lecture.	agree | disagree | not sure
2	I know how long a lecture usually is.	agree | disagree | not sure
3	I know why students go to lectures.	agree | disagree | not sure
4	I know what students are supposed to do in a lecture.	agree | disagree | not sure

What types of listening do you do at university?

At university there are many situations where you will listen to different speakers. Some of these situations will be academic, where you will listen to your lecturers and tutors, some will be to find information about university life, for example, from the university's accommodation staff and some will be social, such as talking to other students in a café.

In some situations you will listen to one person speaking and in other situations you will listen to a group of people speaking or discussing something. You will also listen for different lengths of time and for different reasons.

Tip ✓ The tertiary education institution you go to after high school can be called different names. In the USA, it is university, school and college. In the UK, it is university, or 'uni' and college. In South Africa, it is university, 'varsity', technikon, technical training college or just institutes of further education and training. In Australia it is university or 'uni' and TAFE (Technical And Further Education).

The different reasons for listening at university can be summarized as follows:

General listening: informal conversations, listening for specific information in social situations, listening for advice from non-academic university staff.

Academic listening: intensive listening for long periods of time to develop your understanding of a topic, listening to explanations of assignments, listening to topics being discussed in seminars, listening to your lecturers in tutorials.

Exercise 1

Listen to the four extracts and write the order in which you hear the following situations:

01

A An informal conversation between students   **C** A student asking staff for information

B A lecture   **D** A talk for students

What is a lecture?

A lecture is a talk given by a subject expert on a particular topic. The subject expert is usually called a lecturer. A lecture often takes place in a large room or lecture hall/theatre and is attended by a large number of students, sometimes hundreds. The lecturer will talk about a particular topic to all the students who will take notes. A lecture normally lasts around 45 minutes to an hour.

The purpose of lectures

Lectures are talks which give students a general overview of a topic. For example, a lecture on the anatomy of the brain will give you general information about the parts which make up the brain. Similarly, a talk on marketing ethics will give you general information on what 'marketing ethics' means along with information on current ideas on the topic. A lecture is meant to be an overview. It is up to you to research the topic in detail both before and after the lecture. The lecture is intended to give you a starting point for further study.

How is a lecture different from other forms of speaking?

Glossary

real time
If something
is done in real
time, there is
no noticeable
delay between
the action and
its effect or
consequence.

concentrate
If you
concentrate on
something you
give all your
attention to it.

A lecture is a specific type of speaking and differs from other types of speaking such as a conversation or a discussion. Below are some of the features of a lecture.

1   The lecturer has prepared what s/he is going to say in advance.

The lecturer brings notes and usually has some form of visual material (for example, a PowerPoint presentation) or handouts for students. This means that the lecture will follow a structure and has a more recognized order than a general conversation. The lecturer knows what s/he wants to say and has thought about how to explain it clearly. This is different from a conversation, where speakers think and speak in 'real time'.

2   The lecturer speaks for a long time.

In a lecture the lecturer usually speaks for an hour, sometimes longer. This means that the listeners have to concentrate hard on one speaker for a long period of time. This is not like conversations or discussions where the speakers share the talking and listening time.

3   The students do not usually ask questions.

In conversation or discussion the speakers can interrupt each other to ask questions, explain words, or give their own point of view. In a lecture it is different; the students do not usually have the opportunity to ask questions during the lecture except at the end. Occasionally the lecturer will invite questions during the lecture, but this is not always the case.

Exercise 2

Listen to two lecturers speaking about lecturing, and complete the dialogue.

'Well, I've been [1] *lecturing* for about 40 years now, and it's changed a lot. I remember my first lecture; it was me, the [2]_____ and about 100 students. It was a bit of a scary experience. I've seen lots of changes since then, mainly when [3]_____ were introduced. We started with [4]_____, where I would project slides so that the students could see them, to PowerPoint presentations which everyone uses, and now finally to [5]_____. I'm a professor in philosophy, but sometimes I feel like a professor of technology!'

'I lecture in pharmacy at the local university. The [6]_____ has room for about 60 students. It's got a [7]_____ at the front, but I don't like to use it. I always try to make the lecture interesting. I bring in [8]_____ to help students make [9]_____. There isn't time for [10]_____ in the lectures. Lectures are more like [11]_____, but students can always bring questions to their [12]_____ instead.'

Exercise 3

Choose a word from your answers and match the word to its definition.

1 _____*discussion*_____ when people talk about something, often in order to reach a decision

2 _____ a large flat, thin, rectangular piece of wood used for writing on

3 _____ a paper containing a summary of a lecture

4 _____ a regular meeting between a member of the teaching staff and one or several students for discussion of a subject that is being studied

5 _____ a large touch-sensitive screen connected to a computer and a digital projector, used for teaching in the classroom

6 _____ a high sloping desk for notes when giving a lecture

7 _____ a flat vertical surface on which pictures or words are shown

8 _____ a machine that has a light inside it and makes the writing or pictures on a sheet or piece of plastic appear on a screen or wall

9 _____ a room in a university or college where lectures are given

10 _____ something you write down to remind yourself of something

11 _____ a formal talk to show and explain an idea to an audience

What is expected from you?

Your lecturers will expect you to do the following things.

Before the lecture:

- Do some preparatory reading. This will give you some background on the topic and make it easier to understand the lecture.

- Find out what the lecture is about and look up some key words.

For more on preparing for lectures see Chapter 2.

During the lecture:

- Take notes while the lecturer is speaking.

- Do not talk to other students. Try to concentrate during the lecture.

After the lecture:

- Do any follow up reading suggested by your lecturer.

- Organize your notes and any handouts you are given. This will help with essay writing and revision in the future.

Exercise 4

Imagine you are going to a lecture called 'The Future of Social Networking'. Look at A–I below and decide if you should do them before, during or after the lecture.

A Look up any unknown words from the lecture, or ask a friend.

B Try to sit near the front and make notes. Don't expect to understand everything.

C Try to listen to radio programmes on the subject.

D Look up words on the topic of social networking and check their translations. If possible, try to listen to the words so when you hear them you will be able to identify them.

E Check through your notes and make sure you understand them.

F Speak to other students about the topic before you go to the lecture, to familiarize yourself with the subject.

G Compare your notes with someone else who was at the lecture.

H Write down any important words that you don't understand.

I Try to write down only the key points. Don't try to write everything down!

Before the lecture	During the lecture	After the lecture

Tip ✓ You may be able to record lectures, but you must ask the lecturer's permission to do this.

Tip

Pronunciation: the rhythm of English

Glossary

rhythm
A rhythm is a regular series of sounds or movements.

Standard English is a stress-timed language, which means that the content words (nouns, verbs, adjectives, adverbs) are usually spoken with more emphasis or 'stress' by the speaker. In general the speaker does not stress the other 'grammar' words. Below are some examples of unstressed grammar words.

> For example:
>
> Modal verbs: *may, might, can, could, will, would, must, should …*
>
> Auxiliary verbs: *is, are, was, were, have, had*
>
> Prepositions: *in, at, to, for*, etc.
>
> Articles: *a, the*
>
> Pronouns: *I, he, she, it, they*, etc.
>
> Quantifiers: *some, all, none*, etc.

These two English sentences take approximately the same amount of time to say.

> 1 **Please wait here** <u>and</u> <u>the</u> **manager** <u>will</u> **see** <u>you</u> <u>in</u> **5 minutes.**
>
> 2 <u>If</u> <u>you</u> <u>just</u> **wait here,** <u>the</u> **manager** <u>will</u> <u>be</u> **able** <u>to</u> **see** <u>you</u> <u>in</u>
>   **5 minutes.**

The stressed words are in **bold** and the unstressed words are <u>underlined.</u>

Now listen to the examples.

03

Using stressed and unstressed words is very common with native speakers of English but less common in people who use English as a second or other language. These speakers tend to make less difference between stressed and unstressed words compared to native speakers of English.

Exercise 5

Listen to the following sentences and mark the stressed and unstressed words used by the speaker.

04

1 'Last week I went to a really interesting lecture on space but I didn't understand that much of it because I hadn't prepared enough.'

2 'One of the most important aspects of university study which is totally different from school is being able to manage the workload.'

3 'What I don't like about studying biology is having to write up the lab reports after doing the experiments.'

4 'So, if you look at this slide, you'll notice how the concepts of philosophy as described by the Enlightenment interact with our everyday lives, even in the 21st century.'

Tip ✓ Remember that the rhythm of different speakers is unique so the rules of stress in English are general. Stress patterns might differ according to the accent and background of the lecturer.

For more on word stress and speaker intonation see Chapter 5.

The difficulty of lectures

Glossary

attention span
Your attention span is the amount of time that you can concentrate on a particular task, activity, or subject without becoming distracted.

When English is not your first language, lectures can seem very challenging, but you can develop techniques or strategies to help you focus your listening. Firstly, you will need to be prepared to listen to the lecturer talking for a long time, so you need to develop a good attention span. Secondly, your lecturers will have different accents and some will speak quickly, some slowly. Some of your lecturers will be easier to understand than others. Remember that not every lecturer will be a good speaker, some may repeat themselves, or speak too quietly, or be unclear.

For more on accents see Chapter 4.

Glossary

terminology
The terminology
of a subject is
the set of special
words and
expressions used
in connection
with it.

Also the terminology used in lectures will sometimes be unfamiliar. Often very subject specific vocabulary is used and this means that some sections may be easier to understand than others. Finally, it can be easy to lose the path of the lecture and not understand how one part links to another. All of these problems can be solved with careful planning.

Possible solutions to the difficulties of lectures

Exercise 6

Look at the solutions in the table and match them to the problems (A–D).

A Problems with subject specific vocabulary. **C** Problems with losing the path of the lecture.

B Problems with general understanding. **D** Problems understanding sections of the lecture.

	Solutions	Problems
1	Record the lecture. Swap notes with another student to check understanding. Meet with fellow students to discuss the key points of the lecture.	
2	Listen to long stretches of speech like the radio or online talks. Make sure you reposition yourself to keep focusing. Sit up straight.	
3	Highlight in your notes where you have got lost or not understood, then complete these later with help. Remember that you do not need to write down every word.	
4	Find out the lecture topic beforehand. Find and translate the key terms. Read around the topic of the lecture before you go.	

Formal and informal language in lectures

The type of language you hear in your lectures will vary depending on subject and speaker, but there are some common features in the language of lectures. Some features are associated with academic English (formal features) and some features are more related to spoken English (informal features). In your lectures, be prepared for a mix of both formal and informal language features when listening to lectures.

Tips ✓ Reading and writing in academic English tends to be formal.
 ✓ Even in a formal lecture, language may be more informal because it is spoken.

Exercise 7

Read the definitions of language features in lectures and divide them into three groups: 'formal', 'informal' and 'both'.

	Language	Definition	Example	Group
1	Signposting	Words used to give indications of where the speech is going.	*firstly* *in other words*	
2	Noun phrases	A group of nouns used together to make a long descriptive noun.	*the issue of stem cell research ...*	
3	Idioms	An expression which is familiar to a group of people, but not easily identifiable from the words within it.	*To go out on a limb* (to support something even though it might put you in a difficult position)	
4	Phrasal verbs	A two part verb that is made up of a verb + preposition or verb + adverb.	*find out* (to discover)	
5	Passive constructions	A structure which focuses on the object of an action and not the subject.	*The evidence <u>was tested</u> in four countries.*	
6	Hedging	Words which make a statement less direct for example, modal verbs, adverbs, adjectives, etc.	*There <u>may</u> be several <u>possible</u> reasons for the results.*	
7	Reporting verbs	Verbs which report the words of people.	*A group of academics at Exeter University <u>assert</u> that the results need further analysis.*	

Exercise 8

Listen to the lecture on negotiation techniques and complete the examples of features mentioned in Exercise 7.

05

1   F_____ of a_____

2   It c_____ be s_____

3   E_____ up

4   The k_____ to great negotiation

5   The r_____ w_____ in negotiation

6   A t_____-w_____ street

7   The i_____ choices the other p_____ is making

8   As w_____ as

9   Let's l_____ to

10 B_____ up

Exercise 9

Now label the phrases in Exercise 8 with the features in Exercise 7.

For example: 1 *First of all = signposting*

Tips ✓ Reading and writing in academic English tends to be formal.
         ✓ Even in a formal lecture, language may be more informal because it is spoken. Things like phrasal verbs and idiomatic language are often used in spoken English, even in lectures.

Exercise 10

Look at the following lecture extracts and decide which lecturer uses more formal language and which uses more informal language.

A *We shall begin with an overview of traditional reporting tools used by French newspapers today, and assess whether these tools could be adapted for other countries. Then we will consider how globalization has affected all such reporting methods.*

B *We will start with looking at traditional reporting tools used by French newspapers at the moment, and assess whether these tools would work out in other markets. Then we'll look at how globalization has had a knock-on effect on all these kinds of reporting methods.*

Why attend lectures?

There are many reasons to attend lectures at university. Going to lectures will help you learn new information about your subject area, get ideas for writing assignments, or just give you the opportunity to meet up with other students on your course. However, the main reasons for going to lectures can be divided into two main areas.

Exercise 11

Look at the list of reasons for going to lectures. Decide which relate to understanding your course content and which relate to personal study and assessment.

1   You may get some ideas to help you with your essays, exams and presentations.

2   You can find out about how the topic of the lecture relates to the other topics or modules on your course.

3   You will see how the topic is currently understood by academics in your university and other universities around the world.

4   Your lecturer will focus on the important areas of the topic so you don't waste your time researching unimportant aspects afterwards.

5   You learn about how the topic has developed over time through academic research.

6   Your lecturer may give you suggestions for reading to help you develop your understanding of the lecture topic.

Understanding your course content	Helping with your assignments and assessments

Remember

✓ A lecture is a specific form of listening; you need to listen, take notes, and keep focused. You cannot usually ask questions.

✓ The lecturer may use a mix of formal and informal language.

✓ You may hear many different lecturers. They may use different intonation to what you are used to. Try to become familiar with this.

✓ You will be expected to have done some preparatory work, keep good notes and do some follow-up reading.

✓ You may be able to record your lectures, but make sure you have permission.

2 | Preparing for lectures

Aims ✓ learn to use the course structure to prepare for lectures
✓ read before a lecture
✓ identify key vocabulary

✓ identify 'chunking'
✓ recognize signposting language

Aims

Quiz
Self-evaluation

Read the statements about preparing for a lecture below and circle the answers that are true for you.

1	Read a lot of books about the topic before going to the lecture.	useful | not useful
2	Discuss what you know about the topic with other students on your course.	useful | not useful
3	Do nothing – your lecturer will explain everything in the lecture.	useful | not useful
4	Read about the topic on the internet.	useful | not useful
5	Read a little about the topic such as an introductory chapter in a textbook.	useful | not useful
6	Write a list of things you know about the topic and what you want to learn in the lecture.	useful | not useful

06

Exercise 1
Listen to an interview with Sarah, a Sociology student, about preparing for lectures and compare her ideas with your answers to the Self-evaluation task.

How does my course structure relate to my lectures?

The structure of your course is the order that you do the modules, lectures and assignments. When you start a university course you will be given a 'handbook' which is a document containing all the information about what you will study, the assessments you will do, lists of books and journal articles to read and all the rules and regulations of the university. It can be a useful place to start your preparation for lectures. It will usually give you a list of lecture topics and the books or articles you should read, which means you can start preparing straight away.

Tips The reading list for your course may be long. It is usually divided into two sections; core and supplementary reading.

✓ Start with the core reading as this gives a solid foundation to the course or module.
✓ Look at the supplementary reading when you have a better idea of the topic.

Exercise 2

Look at this section of a contents page from an undergraduate Sociology degree handbook and answer the questions.

1 Which modules will be a general overview of a topic? How do you know?

2 Which modules do you think a first year Sociology student would need to do more preparation for? Why?

First Year Sociology Modules	Page
1 Introduction to Sociology	10
2 Theories in Sociology	11
3 Modern community structures	12
4 Introduction to social welfare	13
5 The principles of social welfare	14
6 Social welfare in practice	15

Tip ✓ Modules based on principles may be more complicated so you may need to prepare more to get the most out of the lecture.

Exercise 3

Imagine that you are a Sociology degree student. Look at the reading list from the course handbook. Decide which book or article you should read before each of the lectures in the handbook. You will need to use two of the books/articles more than once.

Reading list BA Business Studies – First year modules

Brown, S. and Cross, J. (2008) Understanding the reality of social welfare. Oxford: Oxford Publishing. **CHAPTER 1**

Fredrickson, U. (2002) Social welfare; origins, theorizing and applicability. Richmond House Publishing: New York. **CHAPTERS 1 and 6**

Thomas, F. (2010) Introduction to theories and ideas in Sociology, London: McGraw Hill Education. **UNITS 1–3**

Walters, G. (1999) How new communities work in the 21st century. Journal of Globalisation Vol 1 (5) p. 234–240

Module 1: Introduction to Sociology

Book(s)/ article: _____

Module 2: Theories in Sociology

Book(s)/ article: _____

Module 3: Modern community structures

Book(s)/ article: _____

Module 4: Introduction to social welfare

Book(s)/ article: _____

Module 5: The principles of social welfare

Book(s)/ article: _____

Module 6: Social welfare in practice

Book(s)/ article: _____

Reading as a way to prepare for lectures

Reading is a good way to prepare for lectures because it means you can develop a general understanding of the information your lecturer will talk about. When you read about a topic you should:

- Re-read as many times as you need to.

- Look up unknown words in a dictionary.

- Listen to these words using an online dictionary.

- Ask another student to help you understand the text.

- Make notes on points you do and do not understand.

- Become familiar with key vocabulary and ideas before the lecture.

Exercise 4

Look at the list above and answer the following questions.

1 Which of the activities do you do already?
2 Which ones might you find useful?
3 Why could they be useful?

What should I read before each lecture?

Knowing what to read before a lecture can be easy if your lecturers give you particular books or articles before each lecture. However, if no reading list is provided, you will need to make one yourself.

Exercise 5

Imagine you are going to a politics lecture called 'The impact of print, online and visual media on election results in EU countries post 2000'. Read the description of the lecture. Write a list of six things you could do or read before the lecture.

This lecture will look at how the three types of media have affected election results in the countries of the EU. It will examine countries where the media has influenced results considerably and countries where the media has had less impact. The lecture will only focus on results post 2000 and will focus particularly on comparing the effect of online media with the more traditional types of print and visual media.

1 *look up definitions and examples of each type of media*

Exercise 6

Now listen to James, a politics lecturer, giving some advice on preparing for this lecture. Tick the things he suggests. Can you think of any more ideas to add to this list?

07

Advice	✓ if James says it is a good idea
Focus your reading on the specific lecture topic.	
Try to understand the new terminology 100%.	
Check the meaning of new words or phrases in a dictionary.	
Read around the topic.	
Restrict your reading to one or two chapters of a book.	
Try to work out the connection between the topics in the title.	

Exercise 7

James describes a three-step technique to prepare for lectures. Now listen to Sarah from Exercise 1 describing her technique and put the stages below in the correct order. Write 1–5 next to the stages.

08

A   Reserve books on the library database.

B   Asking other students what they know about the lecture topic.

C   Re-read my lecture notes from the week before looking for any connections.

D   Check the reading list for any relevant books/articles.

E   Read the library books for two hours before the lecture.

Identifying and understanding key vocabulary

Understanding key vocabulary is important in helping you prepare for lectures. Make sure you read any information which describes the lecture content beforehand and check the meaning of specific vocabulary. If you find it difficult to understand dictionary definitions, make sure you ask other students or your lecturers.

For example:

Lecture 2.1 - Foundations of Psychology

This lecture will cover the following:

- core areas of research such as cognitive, developmental, social and biological sociology.

- an overview of the conceptual foundations and historical development of psychology.

| the things on which it is based |

| relating to the mental process involved in knowing, learning, and understanding things |

| processes and states that occur in the bodies and cells of living things |

| related to ideas and concepts formed in the mind |

The student here has written definitions next to any difficult words. Think of other things from the previous exercises that could help the student prepare.

Exercise 8

Complete the table with the correct word from the box.

Core module		Core textbook		Course outline		Elective	
Handbook		Journal		Optional module		Reading list	

Function	Word	Function	Word
a book containing all information about a university course	1 *handbook*	a short description of the content of a course	5
a course which all students must study	2	a list of books for a course or module	6
an academic magazine containing a variety of articles on the same subject	3	a course on a degree which students can choose to study	7
a course unrelated to a degree which students can choose to study	4	a book which all students must read for a course	8

Tip ✓ Universities, faculties or departments may use slightly different terminology so make sure you check the meanings used for your course.

Tip

Why do lecturers pause when speaking?

All speakers pause and this includes university lecturers. Lectures may pause for several reasons such as:

1 To allow students more time to write notes.

2 To give students time to think about and/or understand complex information.

3 To check their own notes.

4 To consider how best to explain something.

5 To give students time to look at visual information.

6 To check students have understood something.

7 To ask a question in an interactive lecture.

These pauses usually occur at the end of a sentence, section or piece of information and help students to follow what the lecturer is saying.

Tip ✓ Sometimes the lecturer will change the direction of their talk because something distracts them or they have a new idea. This can happen mid-sentence and usually the lecturer will need to start their sentence again.

Exercise 9

Read the transcript from a politics lecture and mark where you think the speaker will pause.

pause

So, can everyone see the systems on this slide clearly? Is that better now?/Okay, great. Now what I want to talk about here is how this first one is used by the government to predict the popularity levels of their policies in online surveys. This is a key issue for political parties and something that political analysts and bureaucrats have been struggling with for years. You see there is a trade-off between asking the questions and putting ideas into people's heads. What do you think this might be? Exactly, the positive results of one set of survey data may cause negative results in another set as each survey is sent to a specific target group. Surveys require specialist researchers to compile and analyse them which costs money; badly formed surveys usually produce data which is of little use to governments, right? So we are going to look at the construction of these surveys using this system and assess some previous results in terms of accuracy and reliability.

Now listen and check your answers. What is the reason for each pause?

What is chunking and how can it help my listening?

When people speak they use small pauses which are connected to the grammar and word stress of the language. Speakers naturally group words together into phrases and these phrases are separated by small pauses. These small pauses help the listener work out how the words relate to each other and therefore understand the speaker's meaning.

Exercise 10

Listen to two speakers read the same sentence and decide who is easier to understand, Speaker 1 or Speaker 2. The sentence is divided into three sections or 'chunks' to help the listener.

10

As a result of studying urban communities in large cities / we are now just beginning to understand / the effects of new building schemes on creating harmony.

Exercise 11

Read the sentences below aloud and mark the 'chunks'. Then listen to check your answers.

11

1   So what we have here is an example of a policing policy which could be responsible for an area's crime statistics, however it is difficult to say for sure because this is a new approach which may require time to provide a clear picture.

2   It's important to remember that demographics are dynamic, by that I mean that people and places are constantly in a state of change, so don't rely on data that is more than 5 years old if you are focusing on urban areas or towns which have received a recent influx of inhabitants.

Signposting

Signposting is an important tool that all lecturers use. Signposts in lectures are certain words that tell you the order or importance of information, or introduce a contrast or addition.

For example, you might hear a lecturer saying 'So after we've looked at the history of the subject, we'll move on to present thought.' This tells you that the order you will hear the information is, first the history and then today's ideas.

Exercise 12

Below are eight functions for signposting. Read the 16 extracts and match each one to a signposting function in the box.

Functions	
A Clarifying	**1** 'So, now we've looked at X.'
B Finishing a point	**2** 'In particular, we'll see …'
C Ordering information	**3** '… by this, I mean…'
D Introducing contrast	**4** 'We'll start with X, then look at Y, then…'
E Showing importance	**5** 'Moving on to …'
F Starting a new point	**6** '… on the other hand though …'
G Summarizing	**7** '… we can see this by looking at …'
H Giving examples	**8** 'So, to sum up …'
	9 'Now, let's turn to look at X …'
	10 'At the heart of this problem is ….'
	11 'Let's recap over some of the key points.'
	12 'That's all for X.'
	13 '… in other words, this means …'
	14 'We can see this illustrated in …'
	15 'So firstly, we'll look at X, and after that Y.'
	16 'Although this is not always the case …'

Exercise 13

Listen to three lecturers speaking. Choose the function(s) above that are they fulfilling, and write what words they use to do it?

12

	Function	Words
Lecture 1		
Lecture 2		
Lecture 3		

Remember

✓ The course handbook can help you prepare for lectures.

✓ Make sure you read around the subject to prepare for the lecture.

✓ Try to listen for signposting language to help you understand the direction of the lecture.

✓ Before you go to the lecture try to understand what function it is trying to fulfil (for example, is it an introduction?).

Bill Gates and philanthrocapitalism

Preparation 1

You are going to listen to a lecture entitled 'Bill Gates and Philanthrocapitalism'. Which of the following steps do you think will be useful to prepare for the lecture? Tick the steps you think might be useful.

1	Read some business magazines.	❏
2	Find a definition of philanthrocapitalism.	❏
3	Read some biographical information about Bill Gates.	❏
4	Find some background information on philanthrocapitalism.	❏
5	Read a book about Bill Gates and Microsoft.	❏
6	Try to find out and look up some key vocabulary on the areas of Bill Gates and philanthrocapitalism.	❏

Now do the things that you ticked in order to prepare yourself.

Preparation 2

Look at the words and decide which you might hear in the lecture. Circle these.

bilingual	billionaire	business
capitalism	distinction	entrepreneur
philanthropy	philantrocapitalism	pledge

Now look up the meaning of any of the words that you have circled in your dictionary.

Preparation 3

When writing notes, students often use abbreviations. There are some standard abbreviations that can be used when taking notes in any lecture. These are worth learning so that you can use these when you take notes. The following standard abbreviations are used in the notes on page 33. Look at the abbreviations and match them to their full meanings.

1	def:	a	because	
2	uni	b	university	
3	w.	c	Chief Executive Officer	
4	cos	d	with	
5	q	e	born	
6	b	f	education	
7	CEO	g	question	
8	ed.	h	definition	

Preparation 4

In addition to the standard abbreviations that students use when taking notes, it is sometimes useful to devise some lecture-specific abbreviations as well so that if while you are listening to a lecture, you hear certain words/phrases repeated over and over again, you can use shorthand. The following abbreviations have been devised by a student and are partcular to this lecture. Look at the abbreviations and match them to their full meanings.

1	PhilCap	a	computers	
2	BG	b	Warren Buffett	
3	MSoft	c	Microsoft	
4	WB	d	Bill and Melinda	
5	comps	e	Philanthrocapitalism	
6	B + M	f	Bill Gates	

Preparation 5

Look at the notes on the opposite page that the student took on the lecture. Notice how the student has used the standard and the lecture-specific abbreviations.

Authentic Lecture

Lecture: Bill Gates and philanthrocapitalism
Lecturer: Jenny Siklos
Institution: Madison English as a Second Language School
Accent: American

13

Look at the notes on the opposite page. These were taken by the student and most of the notes are complete, but the student missed a few points. You are going to listen to an extract from the lecture that the student missed. Complete the notes as you listen. The notes that you need to complete are highlighted in grey. If you need to listen again, you can, but try to listen only once.

Reflection

✓ Are full sentences used? Why/why not?

✓ Why is the last sentence underlined?

✓ Are there mistakes in the notes? What kind?

✓ What can you do if you can't spell a word?

✓ Did you find you could write enough in the time?

To listen to the complete lecture and read the full transcript of the lecture, visit www.collinselt.com/academicskills

Bill Gates and Philanthrocapitalism	17/2/13
Bill Gates	Microsoft founder/multi-billionaire/ entrepreneur + PHILANTHROPIST Involved in PhilCap
Background	b. 1955 Seattle Affluent family mother was a philanthropist too poss influence? →
Education	13 yrs old – Lakeside Prep Sch started liking comps → BG excelled at programming – gifted student Got into Harvard Uni BUT dropped out. BG said that timing/ideas meant he had to start getting into industry. (Doesn't recommend dropping out to others)
Microsoft	1975 started, w. Paul Allen 2000 left as CEO 2008 left completely
~~PhilCap~~ Bill + Melinda Gates Foundation	Focus on aids, malaria, poverty and ed ed in USA Mission: mix tech advances w. people who need it most Slogan: All lives have equal value 2010: talked about foundation w. journalist – why chose these issues? Cos health has stabilising effect. In USA greatest inequality in edu.
Philanthropy	Def: _____ _____ _____
PhilCap	BG: Vaccines one of best investments in giving. (best return + best chance of saving lives) this is e.g. of _____
	Formed by BG and Warren Buffett 2010
_____	What is it? _____ No contact but public verbal commitment People who agreed incl Mark Zuckerberg (Fbook) Info on website Got 100 USA billionaires, now focusing on _____
	WB has pledged.
B+M Foundation	Want to inspire people to give back. Everyone should do this. Q for me: Would I do this when successful? <u>Read Ch. 7 on PhilCap and answer qs.</u>

3 | The structure of lectures

Aims ✓ understand the structure of lectures   ✓ notice unstressed words
✓ recognize different lecture structures
✓ identify structures of introductions and
conclusions

Aims

 ## Quiz
Self-evaluation

Read the statements below and circle True or False.

1	All lectures in a specific subject (Business, Engineering) follow the same structure.	True | False
2	Lecturers usually give an introduction and summarize the information at the end.	True | False
3	All use PowerPoint slides or visual information to help students follow the lecture.	True | False
4	Lecturers need to prepare their lectures and think about the structure.	True | False
5	Some lecture titles can help you predict the structure.	True | False

Why is it important to understand the structure of lectures?

Glossary

process
A process is a
series of actions
carried out in
order to achieve
a particular
result.

When people are giving lectures, they are aiming to communicate an idea, argument, process or description. Lecturers have prepared this information before and therefore the information will follow a logical order, usually the simplest way to communicate this information. When people write essays they also follow a logical order.

Knowing the likely structure of a lecture will help you to know what is going to come next and the direction that an argument is likely to take. This can help you keep your place and follow the lecture more easily.

Exercise 1

Look at the titles of the two different lectures. Use the phrases below to complete the logical order of the lectures.

Wind/Water energy   The past situation   The future of global warming   Oil energy
What is alternative energy?   Why is alternative energy good?   Predictions

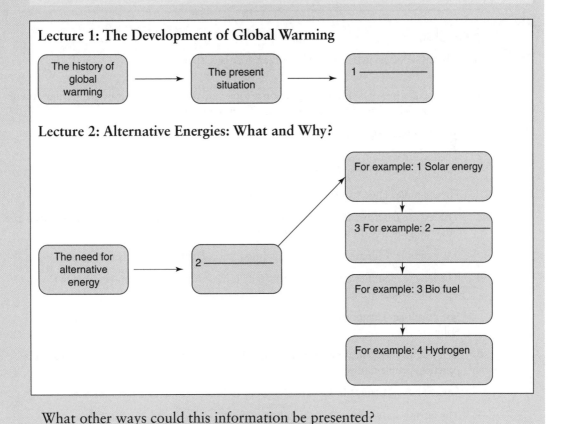

What other ways could this information be presented?

Do all lectures follow the same structure?

Lectures do not always follow the same structure. The structure usually depends on the type of information in, or function of, the lecture. When you find out the title of your lecture, it is a good idea to try and think about the type of information you are likely to hear.

Lectures normally follow one of these structures.

A	Cause and Effect	**B**	Historical/Developmental Outline
C	Argument/Modern Thought	**D**	Process
E	Case Study	**F**	Situation, Problem, Solutions (Evaluation)
G	Description	**H**	Applying theory to practice

Exercise 2

Match these descriptions with the structures above.

1   The lecture presents different views on a topic and discusses how they are similar and/or different. The views are often in opposition or controversial.

   For example: Arguments for and against Stem Cell Research.

2   The lecture explains a specific situation (a case) and analyses what happened over a limited period of time. The aim is to analyse something in considerable detail.

   For example: The Development of NASA in the 1980s.

3   The lecture describes the relationship between 2 things by explaining how one affects the other and discussed the results or impact.

   For example: Climate Change and its Impacts on Early Warning Systems.

4   The lecture identifies a topic, explains why it is a problem and then presents various solutions which are usually discussed and evaluated.

   For example: Diagnosing Diseases in Children – the Difficulties, Complexities and Solutions.

5   The lecture shows how theoretical principles or academic ideas can be used to solve a practical problem in real life.

   For example: Using Mathematical Theory to Solve Traffic Congestion Issues.

6   The lecture shows how something has changed or developed over time. It usually analyses the past and present situations to give background information or make a point.

   For example: Conducting Ecological Projects – Lessons from the Past.

7   The lecture gives a thorough explanation of a topic with details to clarify all parts.

   For example: Exploring and Demystifying Saturn's Rings.

8   The lecture demonstrates a series of actions or steps from the beginning of something to a specific end.

   For example: Designing Robots: from Initial Ideas to Finished Product

Exercise 3

Read the lecture titles and descriptions. Then match the lecture titles with the structures above.

1   Title: The Life Stages of a Star

Description: This lecture explains the beginning, middle and end of a star's life.

2   Title: Mathematical Breakthroughs in the 20th Century

Description: The lecture describes the events that happened during this time in the order they happened. This is so that students can understand key historical moments regarding the topic.

3   Title: The Sections of the Heart

Description: The lecture explains the names of all the parts that make up a heart and gives details on their functions.

4   Title: An Investigation of the Challenger Space Shuttle

Description: This lecture explains and analyses the events that happened in this specific situation.

5   Title: Tackling Ethical Issues in Biological Research

Description: The lecture explains why this topic is an issue. It explains what the important points are and analyses how they can be tackled in different ways.

6   Title: Applying Pragmatism in 21st Century Medical Development

Description: This lecture takes a principle and shows how it works in real life.

7   Title: The Origins of the Earth: Conflicting theories

Description: The lecture presents different views on this topic and compares and contrasts them.

8   Title: Deep Sea Exploration: Effects on delicate ecosystems

Description: This lecture looks at how the first topic affects the second topic.

Time and tense

When you are listening to a lecture, the lecturer will often refer to the parts of the lecture, or the programme of lectures, that is the lectures that have happened, been talked about, or will later be talked about. This helps students know what information has already been given, and what information will be given later. It is useful to become familiar with the expressions and phrases that lecturers use to do this, so you know the order of information being delivered.

Exercise 4

14

Listen to the phrases 1–10 from a lecture on deforestation. Put the numbers in the correct box in the table.

Has been talked about	Will be talked about next	Will be talked about later
		1 *At some point, we'll look at the effects of deforestation*

Look at the audio scripts for Track 14 on page 152. Listen again and write out the phrases in the correct boxes.

Introductions to lectures

Lecturers sometimes give a few introductory sentences which outline what they are going to talk about in the lecture.

For example:	*Today, we're going to focus on the causes of weather phenomena and some of the effects of these, looking firstly at cases of unusual storms and moving on to rain phenomena.*

From this sentence it is possible to tell that the lecture structure will probably be as follows:

> **Unusual storms**
>
> causes
>
> effects
>
> **Rain phenomena**
>
> causes
>
> effects

Tip ✓ If the lecturer gives an overview of the lecture structure, write it down, so you can follow more easily and ensure your notes cover all key parts of the lecture.

Exercise 5

Look back at Exercise 2, then listen to two different lecture introductions and decide which structure it follows.

15

1 _____

2 _____

For more on signposting in lectures see Chapter 2.

Situation and result

Both *cause and effect* and *situation, problem and solution* lectures will tell you about a situation and a result or solution. Sometimes the lecturer may look at the result or effect first and then the reasons for it, however, it is more common to begin with the cause or problem and then move on to effects/solutions.

Exercise 6

Look at these slides from a lecture about bee decline (death of bees). Write the correct order of the slides, based on the structure of situation/result lectures.

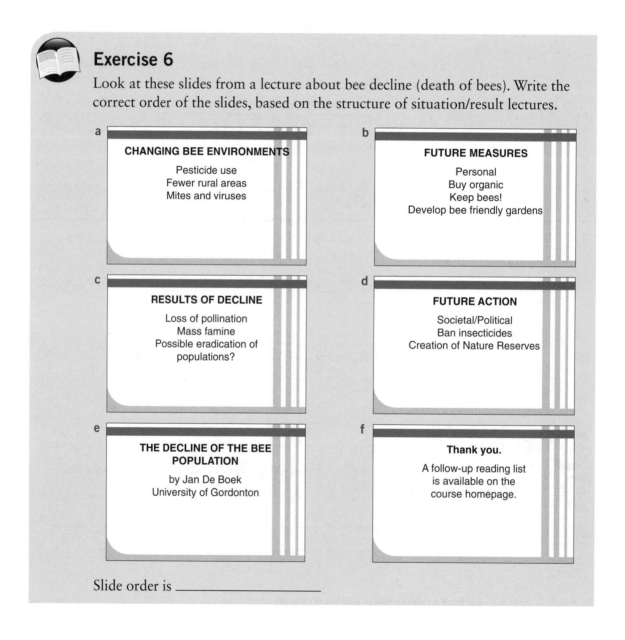

a

CHANGING BEE ENVIRONMENTS

Pesticide use
Fewer rural areas
Mites and viruses

b

FUTURE MEASURES

Personal
Buy organic
Keep bees!
Develop bee friendly gardens

c

RESULTS OF DECLINE

Loss of pollination
Mass famine
Possible eradication of
populations?

d

FUTURE ACTION

Societal/Political
Ban insecticides
Creation of Nature Reserves

e

**THE DECLINE OF THE BEE
POPULATION**

by Jan De Boek
University of Gordonton

f

Thank you.

A follow-up reading list
is available on the
course homepage.

Slide order is _____

Chronological or time order

Some lectures will follow time order. This applies to historical and developmental outlines and processes. This means that the earliest event will be described first and the latest event will be described last. This is called 'chronological order'.

Exercise 7

Look at the slides below. Write the correct order of the slides, based on the structure of chronological lectures.

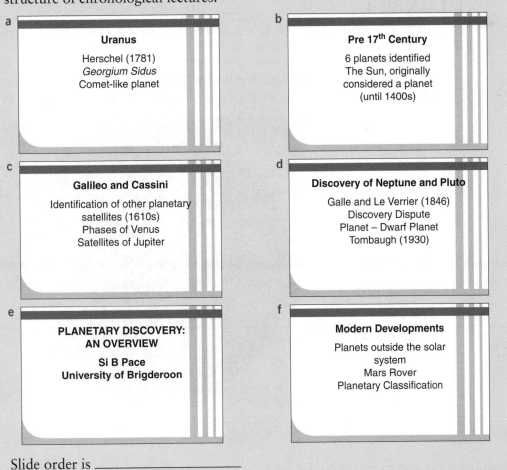

a
Uranus

Herschel (1781)
Georgium Sidus
Comet-like planet

b
Pre 17ᵗʰ Century

6 planets identified
The Sun, originally
considered a planet
(until 1400s)

c
Galileo and Cassini

Identification of other planetary
satellites (1610s)
Phases of Venus
Satellites of Jupiter

d
Discovery of Neptune and Pluto

Galle and Le Verrier (1846)
Discovery Dispute
Planet – Dwarf Planet
Tombaugh (1930)

e
**PLANETARY DISCOVERY:
AN OVERVIEW**

**Si B Pace
University of Brigderoon**

f
Modern Developments

Planets outside the solar
system
Mars Rover
Planetary Classification

Slide order is _____

Describing an object or visual information

In many subject areas lecturers will describe objects or visual information. This may be a diagram or image on a slide or a real three-dimensional object. It is important that you orient yourself (give your attention) to the diagram or object quickly and follow the order in which the lecturer describes the object or diagram.

Tips ✓ The lecturer will often follow a pattern around the object, or they might point to the areas they are talking about.

✓ Patterns for description include, clockwise, (moving clockwise in the same direction as the hands of a clock), left to right, top to bottom, centre to outside. They may structure this around the images or the labels on the images.

Exercise 8

Look at the image of the eye below and listen to the pronunciation of the labels.

16, 17 Now listen to the lecturer's description and mark on the diagram the order she talks about the labels. Number the labels 1–6. Tracks 16 and 17 are from an authentic lecture and the lecturer has an accent from the Northwest of England.

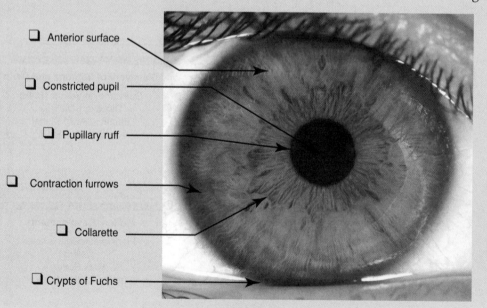

❏ Anterior surface

❏ Constricted pupil

❏ Pupillary ruff

❏ Contraction furrows

❏ Collarette

❏ Crypts of Fuchs

Permission to the use the lecture on The Anatomy of the Eye (Track 17) has been given by Dr Suzanne Hagan and Dr Uma Shahani of Glasgow Caledonian University.

Conclusions

Glossary

pose questions
If you pose a
question, you ask
a question.

In lectures, the concluding section of the lecture (the end of the lecture) can fulfil a variety of functions. The conclusion can summarize the main points, give recommended areas for further study, pose questions to the students for further thought, and sometimes even be the place for giving information about assignments. These are all important areas.

Summarizing – The lecturer may give a quick overview of what they have said during the lecture.

> **For example:** *So, we've looked at the three main areas of research that really impact upon research funding … . First, the relevance the research may have … . Then, it's political need …*

Recommending further study – The lecturer may recommend theories, journals, books, etc. which can help you to study the area further.

> **For example:** *… and that's all for biometrics. If you want to know about advances then please look to Fuller who has recently written about these. And for an overview refer to Chapter 5 in Wolfenden …*

Posing questions – The lecturer may give you some questions to think about in relation to the subject.

> **For example:** *… So, despite a slow start, the field of virtual reality has really come on leaps and bounds… could you imagine what the future can bring? How would you feel about meeting people virtually? Could you cope in a life without human contact? These are the questions we need, as inventors, to think about …*

Giving assignment information – The lecturer may refer to an assignment or essay that you need to do and link how the lecture could help with it.

> **For example:** *Today's lecture might be quite useful for your end of term assignments, especially if you've picked the second one on 'Biochemical Engineering', so make sure you pick up a handout if that's the case. Assignments due April 23rd I think …*

Exercise 9

Listen to the three conclusions below and decide the function of each one. You may select more than one function above for each conclusion.

Conclusion 1: _____

Conclusion 2: _____

Conclusion 3: _____

The three conclusions you have heard are taken from three different lectures in this chapter. Can you identify which lecture they are from?

Pronunciation: unstressed words

Although most of the content of lectures is not made up of unstressed words, meaning can be changed by different grammatical unstressed words. Remember that academic English is specific so you will need to train your ears to listen out for unstressed words in the speech of your lecturers. If you think you hear a different unstressed word from what your lecturer actually said, it is possible that you could misunderstand the point.

Exercise 10

Listen to the following sentence and pay attention to the grammar of the unstressed words.

It <u>is</u> claimed <u>that</u> geologists <u>have</u> clearly mapped <u>all</u> <u>of</u> <u>the</u> fault lines causing earthquakes in California.

1 Which of the unstressed words in the sentence above could be changed to another grammatical form?

2 How would a different unstressed word change the meaning of the sentence?

3 What could they be changed to? Write some sentences changing the unstressed words and explain how this would change the meaning. Use the example to help you.

For example: *It <u>was</u> claimed <u>that</u> geologists <u>had</u> clearly mapped <u>some</u> <u>of</u> <u>the</u> fault lines causing earthquakes in California.*

Exercise 11

Now listen and write the unstressed words you hear in the spaces below.

20

1   It _____ claimed that geologists _____ clearly mapped _____ of the fault lines in California.

2   It _____ claimed that geologists _____ clearly mapped all of the fault lines in California.

3   It _____ claimed that geologists _____ clearly mapped _____ of the fault lines in California.

4   It _____ claimed that geologists _____ clearly mapped _____ of the fault lines in California.

Now look at the answer key. Notice how the meaning of these sentences depends on the grammatical forms which are unstressed in fluent spoken English.

Tip   ✓   When you are in a lecture try to focus on aspects represented by unstressed words such as positive / negative forms, time – past, present, future and quantity.

Remember

✓   The structure of lectures can help you understand the content and follow what the lecturer is saying.

✓   There are different types of lecture structure – make sure you know their format.

✓   Introductions and conclusions are useful to help you understand what the lecturer is going to say and what s/he has said.

✓   Unstressed words can change the speaker's meaning so practise listening to them.

4 | Features of speech

Aims ✓ understand natural spoken language   ✓ identify different lecturing styles
      ✓ notice lecturers' accents   ✓ deal with and record unknown words
      ✓ understand connected speech

Aims

Quiz
Self-evaluation

Read the statements below and circle the answers that are true for you.

1	I find it easy to understand people when they speak English.	agree │ disagree │ not sure
2	I find some English accents really difficult to understand.	agree │ disagree │ not sure
3	I can understand much more when people speak English more slowly.	agree │ disagree │ not sure
4	I try to listen to people speaking English in my spare time.	agree │ disagree │ not sure
5	I try to listen to lectures online to practise my listening skills.	agree │ disagree │ not sure

Exercise 1

Now listen to speakers 1–4 and answer the following questions.

21

A   Is speaker 1 British or American?

B   Is speaker 2 a native speaker of English?

C   Is speaker 3 Australian?

D   Does speaker 4 have a soft or strong Scottish accent?

Why is my lecturer harder to understand than my English teacher?

Glossary

digress
If you digress you move away from the subject you are talking or writing about and talk or write about something different for a while.

intonation
Your intonation is the way your voice rises and falls as you speak.

An English language teacher is usually trained to speak slightly slower to make it easier for students who are studying English language to understand. So, it can be more difficult when you go to university because the lecturers do not normally do this. Here are some of the areas in which the university lecturers' style of speaking may be different from the English language teachers':

- Whereas an English teacher might separate their words clearly, a lecturer will usually speak fluently connecting words together and s/he may speak more quickly than an English language teacher.

- An English teacher often uses language which is appropriate to the language level of their students. Lecturers pay less attention to this and use culturally specific phrases and idioms which may be difficult for you to understand.

- Whereas in writing, order and focus is kept, your lecturers may go off the topic (digress) and come back to it. They may also hesitate, make mistakes and correct themselves. You need to be aware of when this happens.

- You might have been taught intonation in your English classes, but intonation changes from region to region and from person to person. Some native English speakers do not have clear intonation which can make them harder to understand.

Exercise 2

You will hear examples of the four features mentioned above. Listen and match extracts 1–4 with the features a–d.

22

1	_____	a	Fast, connected speech
2	_____	b	Idiomatic language
3	_____	c	Digression/hesitation
4	_____	d	Lack of intonation

How lecturers speak

Remember that there is no 'normal' way of speaking. Your lecturers will come from different places, and will speak with different accents. Some of your lecturers may speak very quickly, or very quietly. Some lecturers will use words which are less common, idiomatic or culturally specific. Some will speak very well and others may be nervous and hesitate when they speak. Also, not all your lecturers will be native English speakers. In fact, non-native speakers are usually easier to understand because they use more international English with fewer idioms and less culturally specific language. Prepare yourself to hear lots of different ways of speaking when you go to university.

How can I understand my lecturers' accents?

Glossary
subtitles Subtitles are a printed translation of the words of a foreign film that are shown at the bottom of the picture.

You will hear many different accents at university; some people will have regional accents and some will have accents from different countries. Understanding different accents will take a lot of practice. Here are some possible ways to help you improve your listening skills before you start university and during your study:

- Listen to a variety of English accents to try to get used to hearing different people. Watch TV and films in English whenever possible, use subtitles to help you.

- You will be able to see a list of teaching staff. Look these people up and try to find out where they are from and think about whether they might have an accent or not. Remember that people are born, live and work in different countries so your expectations may not always be correct.

- Once you start having lectures, identify which lecturers you find more difficult to understand, and then practise listening to people who sound similar (again online, or on the radio). You can listen to university lectures online or talks like those on www.TED.com to give you experience in listening to different accents and lecture/ presentation styles.

- If you are allowed to record your lectures, make sure you do this with lecturers who you find difficult to understand. Then listen again and again, if possible with your own and someone else's notes on the lecture to help you identify key words.

■ Do not be shy to ask your lecturer to clarify any parts you did not understand, but make sure you do this at the end of the lecture. At this point, do not worry about asking your lecturer to speak more slowly.

Tip ✓ Remember, do not panic. Sometimes fluent English speakers cannot understand people with different accents!

Exercise 3

You are going to hear six people giving the same lecture about Artificial Intelligence (AI). Each person will say the same thing but with a different accent. Listen out for the following words.

automation	productivity	outsourcing	atm	checkout	till

Now, listen to the following six people and mark down how difficult you find them to understand, from 1 = Easy to understand to 5 = Difficult to understand. Where each person is from is listed in brackets.

1 (from Australia)   1 2 3 4 5

2 (from India)   1 2 3 4 5

3 (from London)   1 2 3 4 5

4 (from China)   1 2 3 4 5

5 (from the Middle East)   1 2 3 4 5

6 (from France)   1 2 3 4 5

Now, look at your results above.

1   Which accent did you find most difficult?

2   Why were some easier to understand than others?

Now, listen to the most difficult accent again and try to write down the words you hear.

Now, listen to the accent you find the easiest again and write down the words you hear.

Check your writing with the audio script. Were you able to write more from the accent you found easiest to understand?

For more information on preparing for lectures see Chapter 2.

Sound differences in native speaker varieties of English

Glossary

vowel
A vowel is a sound such as the ones represented in writing by the letters 'a', 'e', 'i', 'o', and 'u', which you pronounce with your mouth open, allowing the air to flow through it.

Vowel sounds

The sound of the letter 'a' in some words varies from a short to long sound.

> **For example:** In 'bath' it can be pronounced with a short /æ/ or a long /ɑː/.

The sound of the letter 'a' in some words varies from a short to long sound.

The sound of the letter 'u' in some words varies also.

> **For example:** In 'cup' it can be pronounced /ʊ/ or /ʌ/.

Exercise 4

Listen to these people with different accents say the same list of words.

1 What differences can you hear between speakers 1, 2 and 3?

2 What differences can you hear between speakers 4 and 5?

1 American: cat/ cut/ cot	4 New Zealand: then/ thin/ theme
2 Northern English: cat/ cut/ cot	5 Scottish: then/ thin/ theme
3 Australian: cat/ cut/ cot	

Glossary

consonant
A consonant is a sound such as 'p', 'f', 'n', or 't' which you pronounce by stopping the air flowing freely through your mouth.

Consonant sounds

The sounds of /d/ and /t/ vary from a soft to a hard sound.

Exercise 5

Listen to the differences as the following accents say the same list of words.

25

1	American:	later / community / video
2	Southern English:	later / community / video
3	Irish:	later / community / video

Connected speech 1

Fluent speakers of English do not say words individually but push them together. The words become 'connected'. This causes sounds to be modified in different ways – they may join together, disappear or change.

Words joining together

> **For example:** One of the most important aspects of engineering is …

26

In this phrase the words are connected together because the final sounds of many words are consonants and the first sounds of the following words are vowels. This means speakers connect the words together so that they flow. This makes it easier to say and the speech sounds fluent.

Disappearing sounds

27

> **For example:** There must be different views about this which could have been explored further.

In this phrase the final letters disappear as the speaker connects the words together. In English the letters which most often disappear at the ends of words are /t/ and /d/ and at the beginning /h/ disappears most often.

Changing sounds

28

> **For example:** I'll just let ch you look at the slides … So, do j'you think …

In this phrase the /t/ sound in let changes when it's next to the /j/ sound in you and the /t/ becomes /tʃ/ Similarly, 'do y' changes to /dʒ/ when next to the /j/ sound.

Exercise 6

Listen to sentences 1–4 and write down what you hear. You may want to listen several times to hear every word. The sentences have examples of joining words, disappearing sounds and changing sounds. Remember also that there will be stressed and unstressed words from Chapter 1.

1 _____

_____

2 _____

_____

3 _____

_____

4 _____

_____

Lecture Styles

Your lecturers will have different approaches and styles of lecturing which you will need to get used to. We can divide these approaches and styles into content and delivery.

Exercise 7

Look at the words in the box and decide if they are connected to the content or delivery of a lecture.

use of slides   asks students questions   visual information   reading a prepared script
use of diagrams   handouts   includes discussion   conversational

Exercise 8

Listen to three lecturers giving the same lecture in different styles. What do you notice about the speaking style of each one?

30

Lecturer 1 _____

Lecturer 2 _____

Lecturer 3 _____

Why is lecture style important?

It is important to recognize the lecturing style of each of your lecturers because sometimes you will find that one style of delivery is easier to follow than another. Think about the styles you have noted above. Which one did you find most difficult to listen to? Why? Some lecturers may read and have very little eye contact with their audience, which can make it very difficult to pick up on the key points they are making. Some lecturers may be discursive and go off the topic, which can be difficult to follow. Some lecturers will use visual aids like presentations or models, while others might not.

Some strategies to help with these difficulties are:

- If a lecturer reads a prepared script or does not use any visuals, ask to record the lecture and listen to it several times afterwards to understand the main points.

- With lecturers who speak quietly, mumble or do not make eye contact, sit at the front so you can hear better.

- Learn to recognize words and phrases such as 'incidentally, actually, that reminds me' which show that the lecture may be about to go off topic.

Tip ✓ Trying to get a copy of the slides either before or at the end of a lecture or from the Virtual Learning Environment (VLE), for example Blackboard or Moodle, can be very useful to help you check your notes.

Dealing with unknown words

During a lot of lectures there will be words you hear that you do not understand, either because of the lecturers accent or because you have never heard them before. In these situations it is important to have a strategy.

Exercise 9

Look at the strategies below and decide which ones you might find helpful and which are less helpful. Write ✓ or ✗ next to each strategy.

1   Ask the student next to you to spell the word and tell you the meaning.

2   If you think the word sounds the same as a word on a slide, copy it and highlight it to check the meaning after the lecture.

3   Try to guess the spelling and highlight the word to check the meaning after the lecture.

4   Forget it and just move on.

5   Write down what you hear and pay attention in case the lecturer repeats the word.

6   Use other things such as signposting language to help you guess the meaning.

7   Guess the sense of the word (positive, negative, feeling, size) rather than trying to work out the exact meaning.

8   Listen out for explanations or definitions; lecturers often explain meanings if words are unusual.

Now match the reasons below to the less helpful strategies above.

A   If you make a mistake, it is unlikely that you will find the correct word in the dictionary.

B   If it is a key word, you may understand a lot less of the lecture.

C   This will take too long and you may miss out on something important the lecturer says.

Tip   ✓   The English used by all native speaker academics is typically standard so you do not need to worry about culturally specific words or phrases.

Exercise 10

Listen to the lecture extract and try to write down the words you do not understand. Then read the audio script and check your answers. Which words did you find difficult to understand? Did you know the words when you read them?

31

Recording Vocabulary

It is important to try to predict words that you might hear in lectures, as unlike reading, you cannot check them during the lecture. Here is some advice on how to build your vocabulary, understand vocabulary in the lecture, and record it.

Before the lecture:

- always do some reading around the subject and note down any new words.

- talk about the subject with people on your course. Are there any words that you don't understand, if so make a note of them.

- make sure you have noted down and listened to any unfamiliar words on the lecture topic.

- think of ways you could abbreviate (shorten) key words. Make sure the abbreviation is clear and that you won't mistake it for another word.

During the lecture:

- if you don't understand a word, just write it as you think it might be spelled. You can check later.

- if the lecturer is using slides, check to see if the unknown words are written on the slides.

After the lecture:

- read through your notes and check any unknown vocabulary.

- record your new vocabulary in an organized and detailed way.

There are many ways to record vocabulary, and you need to find the best way for you. Look at the two ways of recording below. Which one do you prefer?

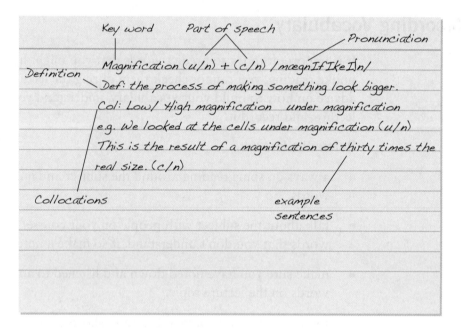

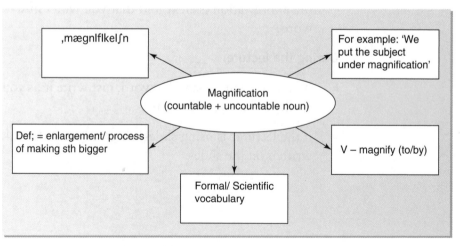

Think about the information you need to record. You might want to add all or some of the following information.

- Definition

- Part of speech

- Pronunciation

- Example sentence

- Synonyms/Antonyms (be careful with these as they are not always accurate)

- Collocations

- The formality of the word

- A translation

- Connotation (whether the word has a positive or negative meaning)

- Different forms of the word

Tip ✓ Try to listen to examples of the word being spoken. You can find this in most online dictionaries.

Remember

✓ Familiarize yourself with a range of different accents.

✓ Lecturers have different styles and you should find strategies to help you get the most from their lectures.

✓ Do not worry if you do not understand every word – develop some strategies to help you manage unknown words in lectures.

✓ Make sure you record unknown vocabulary and continue to expand your vocabulary during your studies.

LECTURE 2

A brief overview of tsunamis

Preparation 1

You are going to listen to a lecture on tsunamis. Before you listen to the lecture, read this definition of 'tsunami'.

tsunami (tsʊˈnæmɪ ◀)

Definitions

noun

(*plural*)- mis, -mi

1 a large, often destructive, sea wave produced by a submarine earthquake, subsidence, or volcanic eruption. Sometimes incorrectly called a tidal wave

Source: Collins online dictionary www.collinsdictionary.com

Tip ✓ Most online dictionaries allow you to listen to the pronunciation of the word. To do this, you need to click on the speaker icon next to the word. Listening to the word and repeating it is a good way to practise pronunciation and will mean that you are more likely to recognize the word when you hear it in the lecture.

Preparation 2

The lecture title is 'A brief overview of tsunamis'. Circle the following points which could be covered by the lecture.

a What people think of tsunamis

b A definition of tsunamis

c A detailed explanation of how tsunamis came to be studied

d An explanation of how tsunamis develop

e The causes of tsunamis

f Some of the effects of tsunamis

g An outline of other natural disasters

Preparation 3

Look back at the points you circled in Preparation 2. Think about which order would be most logical for the lecturer to present these points in?

1 ☐   2 ☐   3 ☐   4 ☐

Authentic lecture: Part 1

Lecture: A brief overview of tsunamis
Lecturer: Professor Bruce D. Malamud
Institution: King's College London
Accent: American (Midwest)

32

You are going to listen to the introduction of the lecture. Which one of the points in Preparation 2 does the lecturer cover?

Listen to the introduction again. What are the three main aspects that the lecturer is going to talk about?

1 _____

2 _____

3 _____

Authentic lecture: Part 2

33

Now you are going to listen the section of the lecture on propagation. A student has summarized the main point(s) of the slides on the handout. For Slides 2.2 and 2.3 the student has forgotten to write the main points. Listen to the lecture and read the main points. Then complete the notes for Slides 2.2 and 2.3.

2.0 Propagation
2.1 Overview

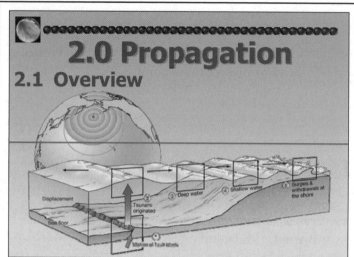

2.1

Earthquake has occurred.

Earthquake generates energy.

This energy transmitted

- to bottom of ocean floor
- then to whole water column
- then to top of the ocean

2.0 Propagation
2.2 'Deep' vs. 'shallow' water waves

- D = Water depth [deep ocean $D \approx 2$–4 km]
- λ = Water wave wavelength
- Deep-water theory: $D > \lambda/2$
- Shallow-water theory: $D < \lambda/20$
- Tsunamis follow shallow-water theory in deep ocean, as depth (couple km) is much less than wave wavelength (hundreds km).

2.2

Deep water theory doesn't

apply to the _____,

tsun in deep ocean follow

shallow ocean theory

bec. _____ much less

than _____.

Figure 2.1 from Thurman, Harold V.; Trujillo, Alan P., Essentials of Oceanography, 7th Edition © 2002

2.0 Propagation

2.3 Shallow-wave theory

c = celerity of wave (speed)

$$= (gD)^{0.5}$$

Tsunami celerity in deep ocean depends on just gravity (*g*) and water depth (*D*).

D = 4000 m: c = 200 m s^{-1} = 720 km hr^{-1}

D = 250 m: c = 50 m s^{-1} = 180 km hr^{-1}

2.3

Speed of the waves =

_____ kilometres per

hour. = speed of a _____.

* REMEMBER THIS

EQUATION FOR THE

EXAM.

Reflection

✓ Why does the student write only summaries of the slides?

✓ Why has the student written numbers before his summary?

✓ What does 'tsun' and 'bec.' mean in the students notes?

✓ Did the student try to write everything down?

✓ Did you try to write everything down?

5 | Understanding points

Aims ✓ what to write in lecture notes
✓ understand importance of lecturers' voice (intonation and emphasis)
✓ recognize main and supporting points
✓ identify fact and opinion in lectures
✓ recognize reference words

Aims

? Quiz
Self-evaluation

Read the statements below and circle True or False for you.

1	My lecturers do not have opinions, they just present facts.	True | False
2	I should write down the references to books and academic papers mentioned by my lecturer.	True | False
3	Lecturers usually provide examples to support main points.	True | False
4	Supporting points are as important as main points in lectures.	True | False
5	I should pay attention to my lecturers' intonation.	True | False
6	Lecturers always tell students what the main ideas are in a lecture.	True | False

What should I write in my lecture notes?

Glossary

subjective
Something that is subjective is based on personal opinions and feelings rather than on facts.

Your lecture notes should only contain the most important information in the lecture. During the lecture you will need to listen and understand as well so you will not be able to write everything you hear. It is important to be selective in what you write. Remember that you can usually look information up after the lecture to check you have taken notes correctly. You can also compare your notes with other students.

Exercise 1

Look at the information which is from a lecture entitled '**Worker Mobility**', (i.e. the movement of workers/employees between jobs, companies, industries or countries). Decide which information you think is a key fact and which is not a key fact and tick the boxes

Information	Key Fact	Not Key Fact
Landmark dates in mobility (immigration) law		
A story about worker mobility in a newspaper.		
The lecturer's experience of moving countries for his job.		
Economic effects of immigration upon the host country		
A definition of worker mobility		
References to books on worker mobility		
A list of the most popular countries to move to.		
Economic effects of emigration upon the country of origin		
Factors effecting mobility decisions		
A definition of work		

What can I learn from my lecturer's voice?

Your lecturer will usually stress some words more strongly or slowly than other words to emphasize that what they are saying is an important point. It is important to notice this and write down the point. Do not mistake an important point for hesitation.

Exercise 2

1   Listen to the following speaker and underline the key points.

2   Why did you choose those words and phrases?

> '*So, the real question is what indicators should a country pay attention to … What indicators show economic decline? Some commentators have claimed that unexpected dips in the stock market are one of the key predictors, but this instability is really quite insufficient as an indicator. Why? Because there have been quite a few stock market falls in the last 60 odd years, with no real effect for a nation. The real indicator is the yield curve … an inverted yield curve often signals decline, as short-term interest rates exceed long-term rates …*'

Main and supporting points

Lectures contain main points (key important points) and supporting points (less important information). Look at the PowerPoint presentation slide in Exercise 4. You can see how the main and supporting points are written on the slide. The subject is the title and the main points are the numbered points. This is normally the case in lectures. Extra information not given on the slide is often supporting information.

Main and supporting points may be presented with examples and explanations, which do not need to be written about in too much detail. Notice how the lecturer explains the subject and then describes the main points 1–4.

Exercise 3

Read the lecture extract on page 65 and underline the main and supporting points in different colours.

Tips   ✓   Main points contain the general idea, topic, theory or concept
       ✓   Supporting points add extra detail such as explanations, examples, reasons and counter arguments.

35

Exercise 4

Now listen to the audio script and read the PowerPoint slide at the same time.

<u>**Types of worker satisfaction**</u>

Employer driven (extrinsic)

1 Salary and benefits
2 Nature of work
3 Opportunities for promotion
4 Training

One type of worker satisfaction is based on employer drivers – these are the things that employers provide for their employees. We call this extrinsic motivation because it is kind of outside the control of the employee, they have to take whatever the company offers. So, there are four main drivers here. Salary and benefits are the most important as no one wants to work for free! People apply for jobs based on the money they're going to earn. A close second is the type of work as people want to be stimulated by what they're going to do for 40 hours or more a week. Studies by Smith and Thompson have noted that one of the key reasons for leaving a job is monotony and the lack of fulfilment. The next two are also related – it's human nature to want to progress in life so promotion and training are key factors in making sure workers are happy. This is perhaps why continual professional development has played such a key role in many companies for the last twenty years.

You should write down main points as they are key and you will need to read about them and research them further after the lecture. Supporting points should be noted if they are relevant to you (For example: you may wish to note examples or studies done if you want to find out more).

Exercise 5

1 Look at and listen to the following lecture excerpt and complete the slide.

36

> 'So, there are a few forms of company structure which we are going to look at today. The first step on the business ladder, so to speak is being a sole trader or partnership – this is where one or two people work in a business, but importantly they aren't a company – they're liable for their own losses. Then there are limited liability companies. This is quite common – these can be public or private and lastly, we've got co-operatives, which we'll talk more about in the next session as they can be quite complex.'

> TYPE OF COMPANY STRUCTURE

2 Now listen to the following lecture excerpt and complete the slide.

> TARGETING VIRAL MARKETING

How can I know what is fact and opinion?

It can be difficult to know when your lecturers are presenting facts or their opinions or the opinions of other people. However there are some things you can listen for to help you identify fact or opinion.

Fact	Opinion
use of the present simple	phrases – 'in my view', 'according to'
findings from research	verbs – 'think', 'believe', 'suggest', 'claim'
theories which have been proven	discussion of research
verbs – 'shows', 'demonstrate', 'establish'	evaluation of research

Exercise 6

Read the following extract from a lecture on corporation tax and highlight the factual information and the lecturer's opinion.

'In the UK, the tax rate for corporations is 20% of profits. There are a number of ways in which corporations can reduce their tax bill but all companies pay corporation tax unless they make a loss in any given tax year. However, the way in which the system works has been heavily criticized by Taylor. According to Taylor we need to think more carefully about how the taxation rules work in practice, especially related to growth in small businesses overall. Although Sachs's theory can apply here, certain economists believe that Sachs has overlooked some fundamental calculations. The interpretations from other economists suggest that small businesses should expect slower growth in all economic climates but to my mind this is an incomplete picture and needs further clarification.'

What helped you identify the factual information and the opinions?

Exercise 7

Now listen to extracts 1–3 and decide if the lecturer is presenting fact or opinion. Write Fact or Opinion for each extract.

37

1 _____

2 _____

3 _____

Pronunciation: Intonation and emphasis

Intonation is the pattern or tone of someone's voice which is used to communicate some meaning to their listeners. From a speaker's intonation we can often understand how someone feels about something. Intonation can give us more information than just the speaker's words.

Exercise 8

Listen to the same sentence said three times. Notice the intonation of the speaker and match it to the feelings being expressed.

Speaker 1: _____

Speaker 2: _____

Speaker 3: _____

A   he supports the idea

B   he is excited about the idea

C   he has doubts about the idea

Using intonation to show opinions

Lecturers may use intonation to give their opinions on theories and ideas of the past and present, the work of other academics and possible explanations to complex areas in their field which have not been proven. Some of the feelings lecturers may try to communicate by using intonation are:

1   scepticism

2   disagreement

3   doubt

4   enthusiasm/ excitement

5   respect

Exercise 9

Match the words in 1–5 with the definitions A–E.

A   objecting to something

B   to have a good opinion of someone's character or ideas

C   a great eagerness to be involved in an activity you like

D   to not really believe that something is true

E   to be uncertain about something

Tip ✓ Be aware of scepticism expressed by intonation. It is culturally acceptable in Western
academic English speaking cultures to express this feeling.

Using word stress to show opinion or importance

Lecturers often want to emphasize specific points during lectures to show
that they are important and students should write these points down or
research them further. In addition, there is a lot of information in a lecture
and using intonation and/or word stress is a technique which lecturers use
to help students pay attention to specific points, ideas, facts, numbers, etc.

39

Listen to the following sentence said *with* and *without* emphasis.

1   Although economists think we know a lot about market behaviour, if
we are truly honest we have no idea how significant even the smallest
changes are.

2   Although economists **think** we know a lot about market behaviour, if
we are **truly honest** we have **no idea** how significant even the **smallest**
changes are.

Glossary

emphasis
Emphasis is a
special or extra
importance that
is given to an
activity or to a
part or aspect of
something.

In number 1 students may miss the importance of the lecturer's point as
the speaker does not emphasize any words. However, in number 2 the
lecturer adds emphasis to demonstrate the significance of what she is
saying. By using word stress the lecturer is showing the information is
perhaps not what the students are expecting; it is surprising or different,
so they should pay attention to these points.

Exercise 10

Read the sentences 1–3 and mark where you think the lecturer will add emphasis and say why. Then listen to check. Use the example to help you.

For example:

*Entrepreneurship is **without a doubt** going to become **the** key aspect of economic growth **both** developed and developing economies.*

Why are these words stressed?

a **without a doubt** – some people do doubt this but the lecturer does not.

b **the** – maybe the students think there are other key aspects but the lecturer does not.

c **both** – some people think this is true for one group of countries but the lecturer thinks it is true for both.

1 The long term economic effects of improved technology in the workplace are especially hard to predict as we currently have no way of knowing whether new and small companies will have enough resources to embrace them.

2 While it is still not entirely clear how social networking will affect corporate policy, one thing we are sure of is that, in theory at least, there will be some measurable effect.

3 The budget deficit of many countries has now become so large that many of them will be forced to think again on whether subsidies in certain industries such as agriculture and transportation are really effective.

Emphasis on unstressed words: modals and negatives

Sometimes lecturers stress modal forms and negatives, even though these are often unstressed words in connected speech. This is to draw the students' attention to something unusual or something which has been discovered which the academic community did not know until now.

Exercise 11

Listen to the examples below and underline the words stressed for emphasis.

1 'Okay, so interestingly, Jones and Franklin at Colombia University wrote an algorithm which could accurately predict share variation with little market data despite people thinking this was not going to be possible at that time.'

2 'For some years now human resources experts have thought that there must be better ways of assessing candidate suitability than the traditional interview and that companies have to spend more resources in this area.'

Exercise 12

Listen to the examples again. How does the stress change the speaker's meaning? Choose A, B or C.

1 a It shows that the formula written by Jones and Franklin did not work in reality.

 b It draws students' attention to the achievement of Jones and Franklin in its historical context.

 c It highlights the difficulty of the work done by Jones and Franklin.

2 a It shows students that this is a serious issue and that there needs to be more work done in this area.

 b It advises companies to change their systems as soon as possible.

 c It demonstrates a new idea that the lecturer feels strongly about.

For more on connected speech see Chapter 4.

Reference words

Glossary

refer
If a word refers to a particular thing, situation, or idea, it describes in some way.

Lecturers use reference words such as 'they', 'he', 'we', 'it', 'this', 'that', 'these' to avoid repeating nouns or ideas. Reference words help to maintain the speaker's flow. When listening to lectures it is important to recognize what these words refer to so that you can follow the content of the lecture.

Tip ✓ Reference words and pronouns can help you link together ideas and understand who or what the lecturer is referring to. It is useful to know these to link up your notes, but remember that noting key ideas is your priority.

Exercise 13

Read the lecture extract below and identify the nouns or ideas that the underlined words refer to.

'Grey and Walters have demonstrated the relevance of risk analysis for large corporations. *They* have shown that *it* is far more important in growing and protecting companies than *we* previously thought. The main reason for focusing on risk analysis is to be properly prepared. *This* means identifying possible problems and developing a strategic plan to tackle *them*. *This* can make all the difference in financial projections and ensure that the company is aware of the kinds of risks *it* might be exposed to.'

1   They = *Grey and Walters*

2   it = _____

3   This = _____

4   them = _____

5   This = _____

6   it = _____

7   What does **we** in line 3 refer to? _____

Personal Pronouns

It is important to know which people a lecturer is referring to when they use personal pronouns ('we', 'you', 'they', 'our', 'their', etc) which do not refer to specific individuals or groups of people.

- **We/ our/ us** can refer to academics in general OR people in general OR the academics in a specific university or department OR the students and the lecturer on a particular course.

- **You/ your** can refer to the students in the lecture OR people in general.

- **They/ their** can refer to academics in general OR people in general.

For example:

1 *The following calculation can be used to work out the value of a company.* **You** *will be using it when you cover business planning.* **You** = the students in the lecture.

2 *Stanning's theory of leadership can be applied to small and large organizations.* **We** *have been studying the impact of this theory for ten years or so.* **We** = academics in general.

3 *Marketing is an integrated part of business development nowadays in fact it underpins much of wider society too.* **You** *can see it in many aspects of daily life.* **You** = people in general.

4 *Here at UCF there is considerable research done into employee motivation and* **we** *use this research to find out what causes employees to be effective.* **We** = the academics in this university.

Exercise 14

Listen to extracts 1–3. What does the pronoun refer to in each extract?

42

1 We = _____

2 You = _____

3 We / you / we = _____

Remember

✔ Your notes should cover the main points and only the supporting points that may help you in your study. Don't write everything.

✔ Listening to the word stress of the lecturer and looking at slide content can help you identify main points.

✔ It is useful to identify what is fact and what is opinion. This can be done using the lecturer's tone and choice of words.

✔ The lecturer will use lots of referring words and pronouns during the lecture. Try to follow these as much as possible, but do not let them distract you from main points.

6 | Thinking critically

Aims ✓ evaluate arguments and views in a lecture
✓ understand the lecturer's perspective
✓ apply critical thinking
✓ connected speech and the 'schwa'
✓ recognize rhetorical questions

Aims

? Quiz
Self-evaluation

Read the statements below and circle True or False.

1	My lecturer has no opinion of the subject.	True | False
2	Academic study is objective.	True | False
3	I must always accept other people's ideas as correct.	True | False
4	It is useful to evaluate information.	True | False
5	I should only describe what others think and not question it.	True | False
6	My lecturer will tell me what to think.	True | False

Why does my lecturer give me so much information?

Glossary

critique
A critique is a written examination and judgement of a situation or of a person's work or ideas.

Your lecturer will usually talk to you for about an hour. This gives the lecturer time to give you a broad overview of the subject they are talking about. When you study a subject, it is important to have this broad overview. It helps you to know what academics researched and discovered in the past, what is important in your field of study nowadays and what the key research questions for your lecturers and you are. Your lecturer will only give an overview in a lecture because there is not enough time to go into a topic in great detail. Also, it is your responsibility to follow up on the points raised in a lecture by doing your own independent research. Within this, you will study some sections in depth, perhaps for essays or presentations. It is possible that the sections you study in depth are not the same as other students, so the lecturer needs to make sure everyone has a starting point for further study.

A lecture covers main points, often with explanations, examples, theories and critiques. You must decide which parts you need to make notes on. Main points should always be noted, as well as points relating to your direct study, for example: your essays or presentations.

You will then need to independently read and research around the subject, paying particular attention to your in-depth areas.

Tip ✓ Take your lecture notes with you to the library to help you focus your research on the key aspects you need more information on.

Exercise 1

Yuen, Samuel and Mohammed are all studying for a business degree. Look at their essay titles below and then read the lecture handout. Which areas in the lecture should they pay particular attention?

Yuen: Examine the effects of the internet on traditional high street stores.

Samuel: What marketing mix makes a successful store?

Mohammed: Outline how the British high street has changed over the past 50 years. How might they continue to change?

Lecture 1: An introduction to retail management

Section 1 – What is retail management?

Section 2 – Global retail management – an overview of regional differences

Section 3 – Case study 1: Retail in Saudi Arabia

Section 4 – Case study 2: Retail in the UK

Section 5 – An overview of key marketing strategies

Section 6 – Challenges for retail

  i)   Global competition

  ii) Online stores

  iii) Costs and pricing

How can I analyse the views given in my lectures?

Glossary

ideology
An ideology is a set of beliefs, especially political beliefs on which people, parties, or countries base their actions.

discredit
To discredit an idea or evidence means to make it appear false or not certain.

disprove
To disprove an idea, belief, or theory means to show that it is not true.

objective
If someone is objective, they base their opinions on facts rather than their personal feelings.

Your lecturer may give you different ideas and theories from different writers. You will need to note down the writer and their idea. You should also write down a description of the general theory or framework that the lecturer is working with, for example: if a lecturer follows a specific ideology, their opinions and research will usually follow that ideology. You must be aware of their broad ideology as it influences a writer's position and views.

For example, if a businessman were asked which was more important, study or work experience, their likely answer would be work experience. The answer might be quite different for an academic. This is due to their background and beliefs. Knowing reasons and background to opinion can help understand and evaluate arguments.

Most academic study has competing viewpoints and often there may not be any 'best' answers. Your lecturers are likely to present the different ideas or viewpoints to you in a lecture but they will not tell you which one(s) to follow. Even if they have a particular opinion, they want you to analyse the ideas and viewpoints and reach your own conclusion about the quality of each one. When you review ideas, try to think of how they have addressed competing views and what evidence they have for their own.

The key to analysing viewpoints can be best described by the following:

Argument: Read an idea and evaluate the relevance and evidence. Find sources which agree with this idea.

Counter argument: Read ideas which evaluate the first idea, and think critically about what you have read.

Synthesis: Evaluate both ideas. Which viewpoint has a stronger argument? Why? Is there more evidence for one idea? Does one idea discredit the other? Has one been disproven? How?

Remember: opinion comes through objective evaluation.

How do I evaluate the ideas presented in my lectures?

Glossary

prejudice
An unreasonable dislike of a particular group of people or things, or a preference for one group of people or things over another.

You will receive a lot of information in your lectures and it is important to evaluate it afterwards using critical thinking. Critical thinking is an essential part of university study. To think critically you need to evaluate arguments and ideas. Critical thinking is not just thinking a lot; when you think critically you need to question the ideas of others and your own. Try to test them and identify flaws. To think critically about the information you receive from your lectures, you need to question and test the information by thinking about it.

To help you consider the type of questions you need to ask, look at this example of a thinking system. This system uses specific questions under headings. The first letters of the words in the headings make up a memorable word.

For example:

B.A.R.R.I.E.R.S – Barriers are obstacles which could stop you thinking clearly. By remembering the word BARRIERS, you will remember the types of questions you should ask.

Biases – What perspective does the writer have? Is this objective or does it affect their objectivity? Does the writer have a broader ideology, cultural experience/limitations or prejudice that affects his/her objectivity? Is there any motivation for the writer's argument that is not based on facts and objectivity?

Assumptions – Has the writer expressed that something is true without any evidence? Or is there a cause/effect without considering other factors which may be related? (For example: if not A, then B, without considering C.)

Reasoning – Are the ideas logical? Has the writer shown reasons for the ideas presented? Has the writer presented clear development of the idea? Could there be any examples or evidence? If so, has the writer given examples or evidence?

Relevance – Are the ideas related to your work? Can the ideas be applied to what you are writing about? Are the ideas too old?

Implications – What conclusions does this work indicate? What do these ideas mean for your work? Will they affect or do they contradict other writers or arguments you wish to use? How can you explain this in your work? Can you use it in your own work?

Evidence – Has the writer given any proof for what they have stated? Is the proof valid? How has the research been done? Are there any gaps in the research? If there is a sample, is it representative? Is it large enough? Has it been tested against anything?

Response – How has the writer's idea been received in the wider academic community? Have the ideas been mainly criticized or supported? Are the criticisms valid?

Situation – Which contexts does this apply to? Can this idea work in all situations? Can it be applied more widely or more narrowly? Was the writer writing at a time or in a situation which may affect the ideas or conclusions?

Tip ✓ Select the critical questions that are applicable to your work. Not all of the questions above will be relevant to your study. Scientifically, research will largely be evidence based, meaning that questions about assumptions, evidence and sampling will be most important. Arts subjects may focus more on questions of reasoning, situation and bias.

Exercise 2

You are going to listen to eight lecture extracts and identify different types of critical thinking. First match the words 1–10 with the descriptions a–j below.

1	contemporary	a	reduction in the success of a business activity
2	refreshing	b	living in the same period of time
3	scathing	c	left-wing beliefs or theories
4	downturn	d	section of the population sharing common characteristics such as age, sex or class
5	regulated	e	vague, imprecise
6	socialist ideology	f	scornful, harshly critical
7	free trade	g	international trade that is free of government interference
8	demographic	h	fact or situation that is observed to exist.
9	phenomenon	i	controlled
10	loose	j	pleasantly different or new

Exercise 3

Listen to and read the eight lecture extracts below. In each extract the lecturer is applying critical thinking. Match each extract with the correct form of critical thinking in the box below.

| Biases   Assumption   Reasoning   Relevance   Implications   Evidence   Response   Situation |

Extract 1

'Although Bryant's argument is an interesting one, <u>it has wide reaching effects</u> in terms of contemporary theory and <u>these need to be taken quite carefully into consideration</u>.'

Type: *Implications*   Support/criticism

Extract 2

'Parlour's theory relating to social networks is an interesting one, and certainly a refreshing approach to this relatively new area. However, it has been met with scepticism by his peers. As we can see both Bartlett and Previn have given scathing critiques. In particular addressing …'

Type: _____   Support/criticism

Extract 3

'Although his work states that lack of money is the only real reason for the downturn in high street profits… this ignores other possible factors, which really need to be addressed. There is a mix of causes …'

Type: _____   Support/criticism

Extract 4

'We have to remember that Brudenell was writing this at a time when business was not as regulated as it is today …'

Type: _____   Support/criticism

Extract 5

'We have to remember, that although Garrett's theory is useful, it very much comes from his socialist ideology and doesn't particularly consider benefits of free trade.'

Type: _____   Support/criticism

Extract 6

'Anderton based this argument on the research he conducted, which had a large sample and covered most demographic groups. In fact, it's the largest and most representative survey of its kind.'

Type: _____   Support/criticism

Extract 7

'When you read Yorath's paper, although he identifies the phenomenon of crowd funding, his definition is loose and he fails to explain how he reaches this conclusion.'

Type: _____ Support/criticism

Extract 8

'Charleston's theory is particularly relevant to those of you who are studying marketing in terms of fashion, as the theory applies specifically to this area. Fashion marketing is quite a distinct area in which not all theories …'

Type: _____ Support/criticism

Exercise 4

Underline the vocabulary in Exercise 3 that helped you identify the correct form of critical thinking. Can you think of any other words that could be used to express these forms?

Exercise 5

Look at the extracts in Exercise 3 again. For each one, mark whether the critical thinking has supported or criticized the argument.

Exercise 6

Listen to the lecture extract and identify what is wrong with Dr Burns' ideas. Choose one of the options below to explain what is wrong with the ideas. Then try to note down exactly why the ideas are flawed.

Option 1: He shows bias towards supermarkets and although his reasoning is good for the pharmaceutical company it isn't relevant to the town.

Option 2: Although Dr Burns has mentioned evidence, his evidence is relevant to how the town could grow socially, not economically.

Option 3: He shows bias towards the pharmaceutical company and has made assumptions that more supermarkets make more money. All arguments are based on poor reasoning.

Option 4: Although the pharmaceutical growth has sound reasoning, the supermarket idea doesn't have good reasoning and assumes more supermarkets will bring growth, which may not be the case.

What's my lecturer's opinion?

Glossary

controversial
If you describe
something or
someone as
controversial,
you mean that
they are the
subject of intense
public argument,
disagreement, or
disapproval.

Although academic study is objective, this does not mean that people do not have opinions on academic work. Remember that many people apply critical thinking, which is largely objective, to academic ideas, which then forms their opinion on that idea.

Sometimes your lecturer will make their opinion clear, for example: 'Davidson's ideas in this area were fundamentally wrong in my opinion. This is because of ….'

Sometimes your lecturer will show their opinion less clearly, for example: 'Davidson's controversial ideas in this area …' (Here the adjective 'controversial' suggests the lecturer's opinion)

When you are in a lecture, think of not only the adjectives your lecturer is using to describe theories and ideas, but also their body language, which can help you to understand the lecturer's opinion.

It can be difficult to know if you should agree with your lecturers' ideas. In some situations your lecturer will show you how past ideas have been discredited or that new research has proven an old idea to be wrong. In these cases it is likely that many academics have the same opinion and therefore you should probably agree with your lecturer's opinion. However, in other situations it may be less clear. For example, your lecturer may believe in the importance of government regulation in the banking sector but s/he may encourage their students to form their own opinion on this. You will learn how to respond to each of your lecturers as you study.

Tip ✓ Set up a discussion group with other students. After each lecture meet up and critically discuss the content and ideas presented by your lecturer.

Exercise 7

Look at the list of adjectives below and match them to their descriptions in the box. Then decide whether you think each adjective has a positive or negative meaning in the phrases.

1 Smith's **disputed** idea …   *G negative*

2 Smith's **seminal** work …   _____

3 Smith's **groundbreaking** theory …   _____

4 Smith's **hopeful** concept …   _____

5 What makes Smith's work **questionable** is …   _____

6 Smith's theory could be considered **incomplete** …   _____

7 Smith is very **objective** in …   _____

8 Smith's data may be **inaccurate** …   _____

9 Smith makes **significant** contributions to …   _____

10 However, Smith's ideas are **unconvincing** …   _____

11 It could be claimed that Smith is **misguided** in …   _____

A believing that something that you want to happen will happen

B without emotional or personal bias

C important

D unlikely or hard to believe

E not completely acceptable

F innovative or completely new

G an argument or disagreement

H incorrect or wrong

I not finished

J unwise or foolish

K very important and influential

Exercise 8

Now turn these expressions into the opposite meaning. Use as many different structures as you can think of.

For example:
*Smith's **undisputed** idea ...*
Smith's idea wasn't disputed ...
No one disputed Smith's idea ...
Smith's idea wasn't subject to any dispute ...

Exercise 9

Listen to the two lecture extracts and decide whether the lecturer has a positive or negative opinion of the theory they are talking about.

45

Pronunciation: Connected speech 2

In Chapter 4 you learned some ways in which English words connect together and flow in natural spoken language (words joining together, disappearing sounds and changing sounds). Now we will look at two more features of connected speech; extra sounds and schwa.

When a word ends with a vowel sound and the next word begins with a vowel sound, English speakers often insert an extra sound in order to help the 'flow' of speech.

> **For example:** 'Can you go out and buy us some more bread for dinner'

Exercise 10

In this phrase, we can see that the words **go** and **buy** end in a vowel sound and the words **out** and **us** begin with a vowel sound. Exercise 10 Listen to the phrase and insert the sound which connects the words in **bold**.

46

This theory can go ... only so far in explaining the decisions of the Mengies Corporation which lie ... at the heart of this case study

There are rules for these extra sounds as follows:

- After /u:/ /eu/ /au/ insert a /w/ sound

- After /i:/ /ei/ /ai/ insert a /j/ sound

- After /a:/ /ə/ /3:/ /ɔ:/ insert a /r/ sound

Exercise 11

Look at the following examples, say them to yourself and insert the connecting sound.

1   It is important to go _____ and find out more data on the financial accounting of the company before you _____ ask questions on the audit process.

2   The phenomena _____ of the micro business is something we see _____ occurring in developing economies.

3   How would you _____ aim to study the effect of management change on employee _____ accuracy?

4   There is a flaw _____ in the research in this study.

5   I'll say _____ it again so you _____ are clear about how the theory works and does not work in practice.

6   Although government should play _____ a part in economic development, we must remember that it cannot do _____ everything well.

The Schwa sound /ə/ is a weak unstressed sound is very common in English and occurs in many words. It is pronounced softly and increases the fluency and speed of the speaker. Listen to the two sentences below and notice the difference in pronunciation. In the first example all the sounds are pronounced clearly; in the second the underlined schwa sounds are much weaker. You can see that the schwa can replace many sounds represented by different combinations of letters.

1   Over the years there has been a lot of support for a thorough approach to mentoring.

2   Over the years there has been a lot of support for a thorough approach to mentoring.

Exercise 12

Listen to the following sentences and underline the schwa sound. Then practise saying the sentences yourself. Try to copy the pronunciation on the audio.

49

1   Education is key to developing the workforce of the future and this is recognized in the theories of Jenson which we'll be discussing later on.

2   What we can see from this analysis is that teacher training varies throughout the world except in international schools which maintain a fixed curriculum.

3   Becoming an independent learner should be the goal of any university student as this will raise your confidence and allow you to make progress faster.

Rhetorical questions

A rhetorical question is a style of question used for effect and it does not require an answer. Here are some ways lecturers use rhetorical questions.

A   The lecturer asks a question and answers it immediately.

> **For example:**   *So, what is the real benefit of financial regulation to the markets? Well, there are actually two clear advantages, namely reduced risk and increased confidence.*

Reason for the question: To focus students on the key points and show that there are clear answers to this question.

B   The lecturer asks one or more questions and does not answer it/them.

> **For example:**   *Where will globalization take the economies of the BRIC countries in the next decade? How will these economies develop? And who will be the most successful?*

Reason for the question: To help students to think critically about a topic. The lecturer is saying to the students 'These are the kinds of questions you should be thinking about.'

C   Lecturers ask a question and say that academics in the field do not know the answer.

> **For example:**   *Are the personality traits of successful entrepreneurs consistent across different industries? Are their distinct similarities and/or differences in for example: manufacturing or service based industries? What about the creative industries? These are areas which we currently know very little about.*

Reason for the question: To give students some background information on where current academic thinking is in their field of study.

Exercise 13

Match the following rhetorical questions to the examples above. Write A, B or C next to each question.

1   Can we really fully evaluate the impact of political change on company profitability? It's a question which has been occupying the minds of academics for some time now and one we've yet to resolve.

2   Why do companies need to think about work life balance? Because study after study has shown links between this and productivity.

3   Now, what about the role of technology in small and medium companies? How can it be used to improve productivity? Is it often too expensive? And how could these organizations get investment for technology?

4   What are the main problems of corporate social responsibility? Well, let me put them into four broad categories.

What is critical thinking?

Critical thinking has many definitions. Here are just a few:

For example:

> *Critical thinking is being able to look at both sides of an argument equally and without prejudice, and to critique those arguments.*

> *Critical thinking is about problem solving. You need to understand an issue, think about everything that affects it, and try to work out a solution.*

> *Critical thinking is about taking your thought to more than just description. It's about understanding the reasons, motivations and effects behind an issue.*

> *If you think critically, you question what you read and what you're told. You don't just accept it.*

> *The difference between 'normal' thinking and critical thinking is that 'normal' thinking just accepts and describes, while critical thinking analyses and evaluates. That's what you're expected to do at University.*

Remember

✓ The purpose of lectures is to present current thinking and ideas on a topic for you to evaluate.

✓ There is usually no 'right' answer – you should think critically about the ideas and views presented by your lecturers.

✓ Speakers of English insert sounds between words to make their speech flow more smoothly and quickly.

✓ Lecturers use rhetorical questions to make students focus on particular points in a lecture.

LECTURE

3

The pursuit of innovation

Preparation 1

Sometimes a lecturer will give you a handout in advance of a lecture. You are going to listen to a lecture on innovation in business. Look at the handout below. What should you do to prepare for this lecture? List some preparation techniques.

Module 3, Lecture 3: Company Innovation (R and D)

Title: The Pursuit of Innovation

Definition: This means the search for new ideas or products in the business.

Overview:

The search for valuable new products, processes and services is a strong focus on many organizations nowadays compared to the past. In the past R & D departments traditionally focused on creating and developing ideas inside the company and then protecting them. Modern innovation has seen many organizations moving towards a more interactive, networked and open approach to innovation. This means bringing external ideas and people inside, which has implications for how individuals and businesses innovate. For businesses, it requires rethinking the innovation process and developing a strategy for working with others outside the organization. For individuals, these new models require new roles and responsibilities. There are obviously many legal, managerial and financial issues to be dealt with. Drawing on the research done at Imperial College, Professor Ammon Salter discusses the changes in corporate innovation.

Key ideas

1   Past R & D approaches

2   Modern R & D approaches

3   Implications of modern approaches: Businesses

4   Implications of modern approaches: Individuals

5   Challenges: legal, managerial, financial

6   Research from Imperial College

Further reading:

- *Villiers, J. & Stone, R. (2010) Innovating the future: key aspects of SMART business development. London: Palgrave.*

- *Salter (2013) How researching innovation can predict growth areas. Journal of Management Science vol. 33 (2) pp. 423–435*

- *Draper, P. (2011) Is innovation dead? An analysis of corporate innovation policy and its effectiveness in tech start-ups. Business Weekly Jan 2013 p35–37.*

Preparation 2

To prepare for a lecture think about what information the lecturer is going to cover. Next to each point write 'Yes', 'No' or 'Maybe' to show if you think it will be covered and give a reason for your answer.

1 How to set up a successful business

2 How companies thought of new ideas or products in the past

3 What makes an idea successful

4 Modern ways that companies create new ideas or products

5 What the role of an R and D department is in a company

6 What kind of people are good and bad at R and D

7 How companies protect their ideas legally

8 A definition of intellectual property

9 How to get a job in the R and D department of a large multinational company

10 How companies will come up with new ideas or innovations in the future

Preparation 3

Another technique to prepare for lectures is to look up any unknown words about a subject. Look up the meaning of the following words in a business dictionary and write a definition in your own words.

be aligned with something _____

brands _____

draw on _____

facilities _____

implement an idea _____

implication _____

innovation / innovate _____

interactive _____

model (n) _____

networked _____

non-disclosure agreement _____

R and D _____

Authentic Lecture

Imperial College London

Lecture: The Pursuit of Innovation
Lecturer: Professor Ammon Salter
Institution: Imperial College Business School
Accent: Canadian

🎧 50   You are going to listen to a section of the lecture. Look at the page opposite. A student has taken notes using her tablet but a few details are missing. Listen to the lecture and fill in the missing details.

Reflection

✓   Listen again and highlight/underline any points or words that the lecturer stresses.

✓   What rhetorical questions did he ask at the end of the lecture?

✓   Was the lecturer easy or difficult to understand? Why/why not?

✓   Which of the key ideas on the handout did the lecturer talk about?

✓   Did the lecturer talk about any of your ideas in Preparation 2? Why/why not?

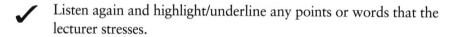

To listen to the complete lecture and read the full transcript of the lecture, visit www.collinselt.com/academicskills

Extract from Pursuit of Innovation by Ammon Salter
http://wwwf.imperial.ac.uk/imedia/content/view/1414/the-pursuit-of-innovation–10-march-2011/

Module 3, Lecture 3: Company Innovation (R and D)

The Pursuit of Innovation

Lecturer: Ammon Salter

What mean 4 indiv.? NOT organ.

Very diff if YOUR job = go 2 get new ideas

Probs = 1   Colleagues NOT like ext ideas

     2   Ideas NOT aligned to company processes

     3   _____

     4   _____

     5   Costs a lot

Result = many org turn away from _____

BUT now = people hunting 4 new ideas

Find rel w/ people 2 _____

Chall. 4 trad R&D orgs

Manage new model = openness

Need people who know:

     1   _____

     2   talk re: IP

     3   know when 2 talk about _____

Indiv have to acquire skills

Our research looked at different roles individuals play in process

Research topic = large org & role of different R&D staff in bringing in knowledge

Findings = 3 roles that indiv. take up:

     1   _____

     2   Some indiv good @ assim ideas into company – enthuse other people

     3   _____

Some-take on all 3 roles & some – none

Result of our res: indiv who take on all 3 roles = _____

Conclusions: Not enough to just explore the ext. space

Need 2 think about how ideas will B assim & _____

7 | Strategies for note taking

Aims
✓ use different note-taking systems
✓ take notes quickly
✓ recognize the importance of relative clauses

✓ use rising and falling intonation to help take note

Aims

Quiz
Self-evaluation

Read the statements below and decide if they are good or bad strategies.

1	Write as much as possible in the lecture.
2	Write down the main ideas, examples and references for further reading.
3	Only write down facts such as dates, places and numbers.
4	Write down your lecturer's opinions on all key points.
5	Write nothing if the lecturer gives a handout.
6	Record the lecture but write nothing.

How can I take notes?

Glossary

technique
A technique is a particular method of doing an activity, usually a method that involves practical skills.

Taking notes is an important part of attending lectures because your notes will help you to remember key information after the lecture and they will provide you with ideas and details for further research. However, many students find taking notes difficult because they are not sure what to write or how much to write. Some students also find it difficult to listen and write at the same time. In this chapter you will learn about the different note taking systems and techniques for improving your note taking abilities.

There are five main note-taking systems.

List: In this system you write each new piece of information on a new line and number each one.

For example:

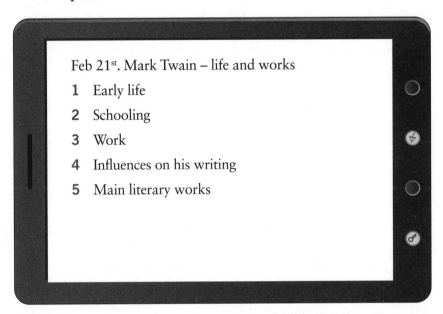

Feb 21st. Mark Twain – life and works
1 Early life
2 Schooling
3 Work
4 Influences on his writing
5 Main literary works

Cornell: Divide the paper or screen into two columns. The left column should be smaller than the right column. In the right column write your notes in any way you want. After each section write a key word or question in the left column.

For example:

Key words/questions	Notes – Feb 21st Mark Twain
Early life	
Schooling	
Work	
Influences on his writing	
Main literary works	
Summary	

Outline: This is like note taking in paragraphs. You number each main point and write it on a new line and then write the notes under it, indenting related information.

For example:

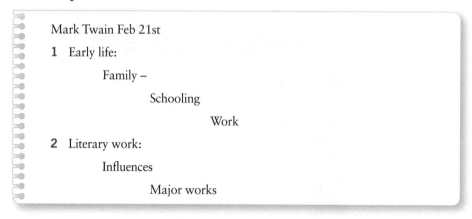

Mark Twain Feb 21st

1 Early life:

     Family –

         Schooling

             Work

2 Literary work:

     Influences

         Major works

Mapping: For this system write the title/main point in the centre if the page. Then write related points around the main idea and connect them with lines, arrows and numbers. Smaller details can be added under these points.

For example:

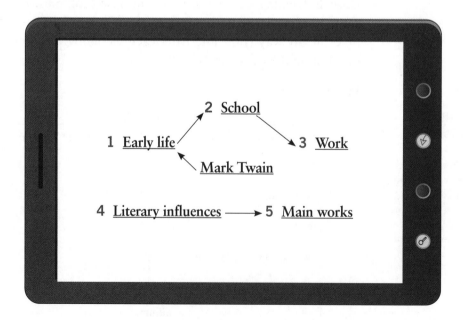

Charting: Divide your note-taking space into columns with pre-written headings and complete the columns with the relevant information. This method can be used when you know the structure of a lecture in advance so you can write the headings beforehand.

For example:

Feb 21st – Mark Twain			
Facts on early life	School & Work	Influences on his writing	Main works

Exercise 1

Listen to Diane Foster, a research methodology lecturer, talk about the advantages and disadvantages of four of the systems and complete the table.

51

System	Advantages	Disadvantages
List		
Cornell		
Outline		
Mapping		

Tip ✓ Some lecture topics may fit one note taking style better than another, for example: a chart is useful for lectures on things such as cause and effects, where you can note the causes in one column and effects in others, whereas a process could be better in a mapping format.

Exercise 2

Look at the following lecture outlines and decide which note taking system you think would be best and why.

1

> ### How to conduct historical research
>
> 1 Primary sources
>
> 2 Secondary sources
>
> 3 Interviewing
>
> 4 Analysing documents and records
>
> 5

System: _____

Reason: _____

2

> The Development of the EU
>
> Creation in 1993
>
> Reasons for the EU
>
> First wave of expansion
>
> 2000 – present: Problems and solutions
>
> Future members

System: _____

Reason: _____

3

> Psychological factors influencing youth crime in the UK
>
> Role models – parents and siblings
>
> Self esteem
>
> Influences from friends
>
> Likelihood of achieving ambitions
>
> Discipline in family

System: _____

Reason: _____

4

> An analysis of Homer's *The Iliad*
>
> ➤ Cultural background
>
> ➤ Storyline
>
> ➤ Main characters
>
> ➤ Themes
>
> ➤ Relevance to modern times

System: _____

Reason: _____

Exercise 3

Choose **ONE** of the systems on pages 93–95, listen to the lecture on Mark Twain and make notes. Then compare your notes with the notes in the answer key.

Listen to the lecture a few more times and try taking notes with the different systems.

Which system did you prefer? Why? _____

How can I speed up my note taking?

Glossary

symbol
A symbol is something that represents or stands for something else.

In order to speed up your note taking either by hand or by typing you will need to practise often. At first you may find it difficult to listen and write at the same time. You may find that you are writing too slowly and worry that you are missing important ideas or points. So, you will need to become faster and more efficient in your note taking. There are several ways you can do this.

Symbols and numbers are also very useful for increasing your note-taking speed.

Exercise 4

Match the symbols and numbers (1–16) to their meanings (a–p).

1	&	a	for	9	∴	i	less than
2	@	b	decrease/ go down	10	∵	j	to/ too
3	2	c	percentage	11	4	k	century
4	=	d	and	12	b/4	l	increase/ go up/ rise
5	<	e	therefore	13	C.20	m	because
6	%	f	more than	14	↑	n	does not equal/ opposite
7	→	g	at	15	>	o	leads to/ causes
8	≠	h	equals	16	↓	p	before

Some abbreviations come from Latin not English but we use them a lot. We call these 'Latin abbreviations'. You may see some of the following abbreviations on the lecturer's slides or handouts, so they are useful to know. They are very common in academic English.

Exercise 5

Match the meanings (1–5) with the abbreviations (a–e).

1	For example	a	c.f.
2	And so on/ etcetera	b	N.B.
3	That is/ in other words	c	e.g.
4	Take note of/ remember	d	etc.
5	Compare	e	i.e.

Tip ✓ You can make your own abbreviations, as long as you can read and understand them. You can also use standard abbreviations (see Exercise 4).

Tip

Exercise 6

Match the abbreviation with the words in the box.

Interesting   Someone   Minimum   Maximum   Problems   Probability / probably
Reference   Answer   Different / difficult   Important   Approximately
Possibility / possibly   Something   Including   Regarding / about / concerning   Very
With   Without   Question   Especially   Because   Information

Abbreviation	Word	Abbreviation	Word
Info		sthg	
poss		re:	
diff		max	
int		Q	
Probs		approx.	
imp		min	
s/o		incl	
prob		v.	
esp		bec	
A		w/	
w/o		ref	

Exercise 7

Now listen to a lecture extract on analysing birth certificates and read the audio script below. Take notes as you listen using some of the symbols and abbreviations from Exercises 4 to 6.

In the next section I'd like to talk about some of the possible problems associated with analysing birth certificates from nineteenth century England. Firstly, it's important to remember that many documents were forged at that time because the early censuses focused on recording names only. Then of course there's the issue of spelling. It's often difficult to follow family trees because of the way names were recorded on birth certificates. The percentage of the population which was literate was low and therefore local officials recording names tended to guess at name spellings, especially uncommon or foreign sounding names for example: French or Dutch sounding ones. This lead to countless inaccuracies in the census but interestingly it increased the number of surnames, for example: we can see the name Smith spelled as Smith, Smyth, Smythe, Smithe, Smeeth, Smeith and so on.

What should I write and how much?

Note taking varies from student to student and depends on the content of the lecture. You will need to develop your own style and prepare for lectures so that you know what kind of information you want to take from the lecture and how much you want or feel you need to write.

Exercise 8

Listen to three students Lina, Gregor and Ozan talking about how they approach this question. Make notes on what they say.

Lina: _____

_____

Gregor: _____

_____

Ozan: _____

_____

Which ideas do you think are useful for you? Would you use a mix of these ideas to improve your notes?

Exercise 9

Listen to the following short lecture extracts. Make notes using some of the ideas from Lina, Gregor and Ozan.

55

Extract 1 _____

_____

_____

Extract 2 _____

_____

_____

Extract 3 _____

_____

_____

Relative clauses

Relative clauses give extra information and lecturers often use them to explain ideas or to expand on them.

> **For example:**
>
> 1 *There are several aspects to gender and language, <u>which</u> is why we are going to spend four lectures analysing this topic.*
>
> 2 *Freud's ideas of persuasion, <u>which</u> have been used by many organizations, are largely considered to be incorrect nowadays.*
>
> 3 *Today we'll be covering the main ideas of Edgerton, <u>who</u> was the first person to come up with a unified theory of social mobility in urban areas.*
>
> 4 *One of the ideas <u>that</u> changed the way we think about the effects of family on success in education and employment is that of Roberts.*
>
> 5 *One of the key areas <u>where</u> academics disagree is the causal relation between education and expectation.*

Tip ✓ Remember that sometimes the relative clause is a necessary explanation and sometimes
it is extra. Often the speaker will change pitch or pause to highlight if the information
is extra. In the examples above, 4 and 5 have necessary information.

Exercise 10

Look at the examples and decide in which sentences the relative clause has
necessary information and which has extra information.

Necessary: _____

Extra: _____

Relative pronouns

56

Exercise 11

Complete the following sentences with the correct relative pronoun ('who',
'where',' which' or 'that'). Decide if the information in the relative clause is extra
or necessary.

1   Brown's theory was quite controversial for its time, _____ is the reason for so
    many studies in this area. *Extra/necessary?*

2   We're going to look at the ideas _____ were developed in the late 1970s. *Extra/
    necessary?*

3   The Greeks were the main group _____ contributed to the development of
    rational thought. *Extra/necessary?*

4   There are many aspects of company law but today we are going to focus on shares
    _____ are actually quite an interesting area as you'll see later on. *Extra/necessary?*

Pronunciation: Rising and falling intonation

Rising and falling intonation can help you with note taking. Rising and
falling intonation are used by speakers to show listeners when they have
finished a specific idea or point or when they are going to change topic.
Below are some important points to remember.

> **For example:**
>
> - Lists: When speakers give a list they use rising intonation for each item in the list until the last item which has falling intonation. The pattern is: rising, rising, rising, falling.
>
> - Statements with multiple clauses: the first statement(s) have rising intonation and final statement usually has falling intonation.
>
> - Asking and answering questions: speakers usually use rising intonation when they ask a question and then falling intonation when they answer a question.

Exercise 12

57

Listen to the lecture extracts 1–3 and notice how each speaker uses rising and falling intonation. Match them to the examples above.

Speaker 1: _____

Speaker 2: _____

Speaker 3: _____

Noticing intonation can help you when you are taking notes using some of these note-taking systems.

List: start a new line based on the intonation pattern

Outline: indent again following the intonation

Mapping: add another point to the map according to the intonation

Tip ✓ For the Cornell and Charting systems, paying attention to word stress is helpful because then you can identify the key facts or important points.

For more on word stress see Chapter 5.

Old and new information

Rising and falling intonation can also show old and new information. Speakers usually use the following intonation pattern:

Old information	New information
Fall-rise	Fall

For example:

Right everyone, we've covered the main events leading up to The War of Independence
Old information
so now I'd like to turn to the analysis of the events.
New information
Many sociocultural theories describe the interplay between politics and philosophy and
Old information
this is important to understand human action and reaction.
New information

Lecturers often use this intonation to introduce the content of the lecture, link to other lectures in the module or to change topic during a lecture.

Exercise 13

Practise saying the following sentences using the intonation pattern shown above. Then listen and add the rise-fall and fall arrows according to the intonation of the speaker.

1   *Today we're going to first recap last week's lecture on key ideas of the Renaissance and then we'll move on to investigating the impact of these ideas on society in general.*

2   *Looking at the arguments for and against electoral reform over the past 20 years, it is clear that there are many which are no longer relevant to modern society.*

3   *Right, I've put some sources on this slide for you to follow up on after the lecture so now let's turn to the causes of the Surrealist art movement.*

Remember

✓   Different forms of note taking are useful in different lecture formats. Use a style which you find clear and suits the lecture.

✓   Abbreviations can help you write more quickly, but make sure you know what the abbreviations mean.

✓   Intonation can help you understand if the lecturer is changing the main point or topic.

✓   Intonation can also tell you whether information in a relative clause is necessary information or extra information.

8 | Understanding your notes

Aims ✓ understand the importance of notes for assessments
   ✓ recognize when to rewrite notes
   ✓ organize paper and electronic notes
   ✓ how to keep notes accurate
   ✓ use context to help with understanding

Aims

? Quiz
Self-evaluation

Read the following student comments and decide which strategies are better. Write ✓ or ✗ next to each comment.

1
"When I come out of a lecture, I go to the café and read my notes again, highlighting important points in different colours." Simon ❑

2
"Usually I put my notes in my folder and get them out again when I need to read them for my assessment." Dorota ❑

3
"I file my notes in different folders for each module." Ali ❑

4
"My friends and I go to the library and swap notes after each lecture to check if we got the same information. Then we write the extra details on our notes." Sumita ❑

Why is note taking important for my assessments?

Your lecture notes will help you plan and organize the research, designing and writing of your assessments as well as helping you to revise for your exams. Good notes will make it easier to plan your research and assessment writing, give you ideas for essays, give you references for further reading and remind you of key points in exam preparation. Good notes will:

- give you general background information to help understand the focus of the assessment.

- help you focus on the areas of the assessment you understand.

- help identify areas of the assessment you need to read/research more about.

- give you further reading suggestions – books, journal articles etc.

- help you formulate your own ideas in relation to the ideas of others.

- encourage you to link your ideas/thoughts with the work of academics in this area.

- give you an opportunity to refresh your memory, review and process the information your lecturer gave during the lecture.

It is important that you *do something* with your notes as soon as possible rather than just filing them and not re-reading them for weeks. The following sections will provide ideas and exercises for re-writing, organizing, checking and using the notes from your lectures.

Should I rewrite my notes?

This will depend on the quality of your notes. When you first start attending lectures your notes may be incomplete or disorganized because you found the lecturer difficult to understand or s/he spoke too quickly or the topic was unfamiliar to you. In these cases it is a good idea to re-write your notes.

Exercise 1

Look at these notes from Jamal, a Literature student, and decide which parts of his notes need re-writing.

Lecture 2: Latin American lit c20.

Nobel prize winners = 5 (Mistral, Marquez, Vargas...)

Themes in fiction

    political hist = big infl on writers

        indigenous heritage = v. imp bec of sthg about individual countries

          Lang, geog and religion also imp.

New style of wr comp to Europe

    Original bec. no established rules

      Trans BUT also ...

        New structures

          Writing about rural & urban life v. diff

For example: 1 Borges & Argentina – Reject Euro ideas

        Focus on good writing

        Explore margins

Reading = Borges: a writer (sthg about culture – check reading list) + some chapters from 6 books

---

Answer

_____

_____

_____

Exercise 2

What might happen if Jamal does not re-write his notes and needs to use them for an assessment? Add some problems to the list below.

1   He might waste time researching basic details which he could have done directly after the lecture.

2   He might not understand what some points mean.

3   _____

4   _____

5   _____

Now listen to a lecturer talking about a Literature student, Jamal's notes.

How can I organize my notes?

In this section we will look at how to organize notes on paper and in electronic format. It does not matter whether you take notes on paper or on your laptop/tablet or both but it is important to have a filing system for both. The filing system should label each set of notes clearly and organize them in such a way that you can find them easily when you need them for your assessments.

Tip   ✓   There is no right or wrong way to organize your notes. Try a range of different systems until you find one which suits your study style.

Organizing electronic notes

If you take notes on your laptop/tablet, remember to make time to organize them after each lecture. Use a system in the same way as for paper notes to ensure all your files are up to date.

Exercise 3

Look at Maria's computer screen below which shows her filing system for her Law degree notes. What should she do to improve it?

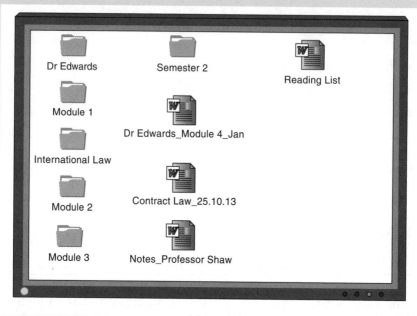

Answer _____

_____

Now listen to an interview with Maria where she talks about how she plans to improve her filing system. Were your suggestions similar to Maria's plans?

Organizing paper notes

After each lecture you should set aside some time to organize your notes. Make sure you have folders and plastic wallets, highlighter pens, module handbooks, assessment titles, and reading lists to help you.

Exercise 4

Look at the following list of organization tasks and complete the sentences with phrases from the box.

assessment	chronological	further reading
highlight	module name	module or topic date

1   Check your notes have the _____, lecture title and _____.

2   Colour code/ _____ any important points.

3   Check quotes have page numbers and references for _____ are correct.

4   Put your notes in _____ order.

5   Put your notes into a folder divided into sections by _____.

6   File _____ titles and reading lists with the relevant lecture notes.

How can I check my notes are accurate?

Glossary

go over
If you go over your work, a situation, or a system, you consider it carefully to see what is wrong with it or how it could be improved.

It is important to check that your notes are correct and there are several ways to do this.

1   Meet with friends after the lecture to go over your notes and correct any errors you find together.

2   If the lecture slides are available on the university's VLE then access them after the lecture to check your notes for errors.

3   Ask your lecturer if you can record their lecture and then listen to the recording afterwards to check your notes.

60

Exercise 5

Read Roberto's notes from a lecture called 'Key Philosophers and Democracy' then listen to the lecture extract and correct the errors.

Key Philosophers & Democracy

<u>Ancient Rome</u>

- Plato BC 4th & Aristotle BC 5th

- citizens should focus on role in soc. – think about money

- majority is imp & democ = most dang form of gov.

<u>UK</u>

- Document = Magna Carta 1215 – said people must obey law.

- Hobbes c16th: Democ won't work, govt should have power.

- Locke c. 18th: contract bet people & govt. Govt protects people & have right 2 change govt

- Wollstonecraft c.18th: all people equal, didn't bel in marriag

<u>France</u>

- Montesquieu c. 17th: limit monarchy, sep powers – basis of US constitution, relig v good 4 soc.

- Voltaire c. 17th: bel in reason → progress, govt good if people prot by laws, democ ok 4 large countries.

- Rousseau c. 18th:

- Rule belongs 2 people BUT people can do nthg – ideas 4 Fr Rev

---

Why do you think Roberto made these mistakes? Read the list below and tick ✓ the mistakes that Roberto made in his listening and note-taking.

1	He did not hear a negative (not, didn't, aren't)	❑
2	He got confused between two subjects.	❑
3	He did not understand the subject of a verb.	❑
4	He did not understand the object of a verb.	❑

How can I use my notes in written assessments like essays?

Your notes should act as a map to help you research, plan and do your written assessments like essays and reports. By using your notes you should be able to review the content, find ideas and further reading and plan an outline for your assessment. Look at the flow chart below which is a guide to using your notes for an essay.

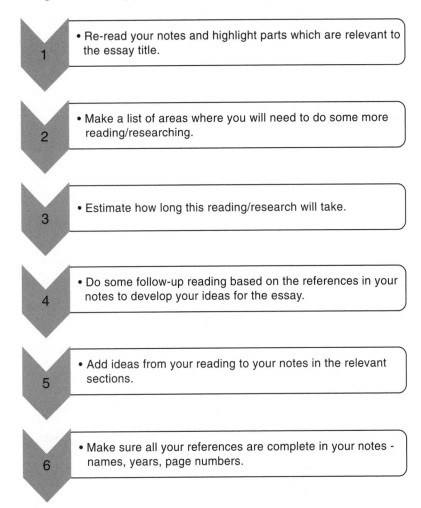

1. • Re-read your notes and highlight parts which are relevant to the essay title.

2. • Make a list of areas where you will need to do some more reading/researching.

3. • Estimate how long this reading/research will take.

4. • Do some follow-up reading based on the references in your notes to develop your ideas for the essay.

5. • Add ideas from your reading to your notes in the relevant sections.

6. • Make sure all your references are complete in your notes - names, years, page numbers.

Exercise 6

Jamal from Exercise 1 has the following essay title as an assessment for his Module on 20th Century Latin American Literature.

The themes of 20th century Latin American fiction were totally distinct from those represented in European literature during the same period. Discuss with reference specific writers and texts.

Look at Jamal's notes and do steps 1–3 from the guidelines on page 111 to show how Jamal could use his lecture notes for this essay.

Lecture 2: Latin American lit c20.

Nobel prize winners = 5 (Mistral, Marquez, Vargas)

Themes in fiction

    political hist = big infl on writers

        indigenous heritage = v. imp bec of sthg about individual countries

          Lang, geog and religion also imp.

New style of wr comp to Europe

    Original bec. no established rules

        Trans BUT also …

          New structures

            Writing about rural & urban life v. diff

For example: 1 Borges & Argentina – Reject Euro ideas

          Focus on good writing

          Explore margins

Reading = Borges: a writer …. (sthg about culture – check reading list) + some chapters from 6 books

Answer:

Step 2 _____

_____

Step 3 _____

_____

Exercise 7

Roberto from Exercise 5 has the following presentation to prepare as an assessment for his Module on Key Philosophers and Democracy.

Choose one nation and briefly outline the views of the key philosophers. Then prepare an analysis of the ideas of one philosopher and how useful their ideas are for modern day politics.

Look at Roberto's notes that you corrected in Exercise 5 and do steps 1–3 from the guidelines to show how he could use his lecture notes for this presentation.

Tip ✓ When you review your notes, highlight sections which could be useful for more than one assessment.

Language: the (noun) of (noun)

Lecturers often use noun phrases such as 'the importance of social policy' or 'a range of accents' to draw students' attention to specific information.

The structure of these phrases is as follows:

> **The/a/an** + <u>general noun</u> + of + specific noun + *clause*
>
> **For example:**
>
> - **The** <u>importance</u> of social policy *has been underestimated by successive governments for many years.*
>
> - **A** <u>range</u> of accents *are used by speakers of English depending on the social status of their interlocutors.*

Exercise 8

Listen to the following sentences and complete the noun phrases.

61

1 _____ is fascinating in terms of how it changed the way in which people in general interacted with works of fiction.

2 When we think about _____ it is clear that they play a key public role in national culture.

3 Bartlett's study of inner city housing concludes that _____ should be studied far more in future.

4 Right so if everyone looks at the slide here, which is _____, we can see some interesting features.

5 Let's now turn to _____ where we can see how he outlines his ideas on democracy.

Pronunciation: Using context to help with understanding

Always remember that the context of the lecture can help you to understand your lecturers even if you think you have misunderstood something. There are many difficulties associated with listening to lectures such as speed of the speaker, accent, complex ideas and unknown vocabulary. However, often the context (situation, topic or information around) can help.

Context information might include:

- the title of the lecture

- preparation reading

- the assessment that the lecture relates to

- the background information at the beginning of the lecture

- specific examples in the lecture

Exercise 9

Listen to the following extract from a lecture. Circle the word you hear at the end.

*When we examine fossils we can tell a lot about how an organism died by its shape in the rock. Let's look at this bird fossil as an example. We can see in the fossil that the bird has extended its legs and is in a very rigid position. This suggests that it may have died on the ground from an attack by a predator and possibly that it died in a state of **flight/fright**.*

Look at the context (topic) in the first line. Which word helps you understand the last word?

Tip ✓ Remember that context can be useful if you think you have misunderstood something.

Exercise 10

Listen to the following lecture extract on archaeological research. There is one word which does not seem to make sense. Answer the following questions.

1 What do you think the word is?
2 How did the context help you understand the meaning?

Remember

✔ Your notes are an important record of the content of lectures.

✔ Check your notes are accurate.

✔ Always do something with your notes.

✔ Organize your notes into a suitable system so you can find information quickly and easily at a later date.

The history of universities in Western Europe

Preparation 1

You are going to listen to a lecture on the history of universities in Western Europe. Before you listen, try to think of some key words that could relate to this subject. To do this, you may have to read around the subject a little. Some of the work has already been done for you. The first five words related to this subject are listed below. Add five more and then find definitions for these words and ensure you know what they sound like by using an online dictionary.

1 scholar _____

2 dialogue _____

3 master (n) _____

4 debate _____

5 Latin _____

6 _____

7 _____

8 _____

9 _____

10 _____

Tip ✓ When predicting words that might come up in a lecture, remember that nouns are usually the words which are subject specific. Verbs and adjectives are quite similar throughout academia. This means that you might need to do more preparation before a lecture predicting nouns. Once you have learned some of the commonly-used verbs and adjectives, these can be used in lots of different lectures.

Preparation 2

Think of what abbreviations you could use when taking notes during the lecture to speed up the process. Make a list of the abbreviations you could use instead of the words in Preparation 1. Remember there are no definite correct or incorrect answers to this. These abbreviations are your own system which helps you speed up the note-taking process.

> **For example:** *scholar*
> This could be abbreviated to *sclr*

(Note: if sch was used, it might be confused with school.)

Authentic lecture: Part 1

Lecture: The History of Universities in Western Europe
Lecturer: Dr Joanna Royle
Institution: The University of Glasgow
Accent: English

Listen to this section of the lecture on Classical Greco-Roman learning and complete the notes below. This time the student typed up his notes using a tablet rather than writing notes by hand.

Classical learning – sophisticated. Avail only to men.

VESPASIAN (Emperor) understood importance of a
1 _____

Learning done through DIALECTICS – still done now (definition: 2 _____)

e.g the nature of _____:"is goodness in single acts or in the abstract?" discussed in Plato's time and today).

> **Follow up**
>
> Look at the answer key at the back of the book. What abbreviations were used in the notes for the following words?
>
> available _____
> population _____
> something _____
> different _____
> people _____
> for example _____

Authentic lecture: Part 2

Note taking does not always have to be organized in a linear way. Sometimes, if it is appropriate for the content, notes can be organized in a spider diagram. You are going to listen to another part of the lecture. This time, the lecturer is talking about life at a medieval university, and the lecturer mentions eight points. Listen to the extract and fill in the spider diagram.

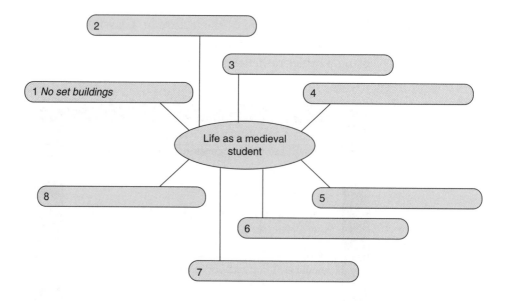

Listen to Part 2 of the lecture again and answer the questions below. Write notes in a linear way.

1 How do we know what life was like?

2 Note down the main reason the lecturer gives, with an example and some of the rules students needed to follow.

Reflection

✓ Did you use any of the words you looked up?

✓ Did you use any of the abbreviations?

✓ How did you find the different styles of note taking? Did you prefer one or another?

✓ Which part did you find the most difficult? Why?

Follow up

How many points did you get from the second part of the lecture?

If you got under four of the eight points mentioned in Authentic lecture Part 2, why? Was it a problem with speed, or understanding? If it was understanding, was the problem with the lecturer's accent or was the language too difficult? How could you improve this?

After a few days, come back and look at what you wrote for Authentic lecture Part 2. Does it still make sense to you? If not, you should think about rewriting your notes after the lecture. Read the audio scripts and note the differences in language in both sections. Which section uses lots of noun phrases? Which section sounds more informal?

9 | Other types of academic listening

Aims
- ✓ learn to listen in tutorials
- ✓ learn to listen in seminars
- ✓ recognize and use polite language
- ✓ revision of pronunciation from previous chapters

Aims

? Quiz
Self-evaluation

Read the statements below and circle True or False.

1	A tutor is a member of the academic staff.	True | False
2	A tutorial is a presentation to a tutor.	True | False
3	I can make notes in a tutorial.	True | False
4	I shouldn't ask questions in a tutorial.	True | False
5	A seminar is a guided discussion group.	True | False
6	I cannot ask questions in a seminar.	True | False

What is tutor supervision?

In the British university system tutor supervision is known as a tutorial and will be referred to as that. Tutorials are meetings that you will have with your tutor. A tutor is a member of the academic staff who advises and guides you on your academic work at the university. A tutorial could be a private meeting with your tutor, so you will be the only student there. Sometimes, your tutorial will be with a small group of other students.

Your tutor is usually assigned to you by the subject department, and the meetings are usually pre-arranged. You may be able to request a tutorial, and your course handbook should outline how this can be done.

Remember, you cannot usually go and see your tutor without an appointment.

There are some key points to remember about tutorials.

- It is important to be prepared for your tutorial. You should go to a tutorial with an update for your tutor on your work, and also a set of questions about your research.

- It is important to show your tutor your written work. Your tutor cannot guess the quality of your work simply by what you say. Give the tutor some of your writing. You will need to check with the department if this work can be emailed to the tutor and when the best time to email the work is.

- A tutorial is a two-way (or more) discussion. Do not expect your tutor to talk through your assignment topics as if it were a lecture. The tutor is there to guide and respond to your questions and arguments. Do not be shy to give your opinion of the academic subject being discussed.

- It is important to understand what you need to do after your tutorial. If you need to, take notes during your tutorial on key works you need to read or changes you need to make to your essay. You can ask to record a tutorial, but this is not usually allowed.

Exercise 1

Look at the questions below and decide which ones are and which ones are not appropriate to ask in a tutorial.

1 Can you proofread my essay?

2 Where can I find more information on X?

3 I'm not sure what to write here as a good example. Could you advise me?

4 Do you think my referencing is sufficient in this section?

5 What mark will this get?

6 I've got lots of assignments to hand in at the same time. Can I hand this essay in later?

7 What books can I read to help me with this section?

8 I don't think this view is valid anymore because of X. What do you think?

9 Can you give me some more information on this comment you wrote on my essay?

10 Can you write this section for me?

How is listening different in tutorials?

In tutorials, the type of listening you do will be much more interactive. This means that the tutor will be responding to your questions, asking you questions, and you can ask for clarification on parts you do not understand.

66

Look and listen to the following dialogues for examples of typical conversations in tutorials.

Asking for Clarification:

Professor Jones: *So, what you need to do is just review chapter 10 of Masterson, and chapter 3 of Rhys-Smith, but make sure you read all of Peterson and Gable's work.*

Student: *Sorry, I didn't manage to write that down. What chapter of Masterson should I read?*

Professor Jones: *Chapter 10.*

Student: *And chapter 3 of …?*

Professor Jones: *Chapter 3 of Rhys-Smith.*

Questions and Answers:

Professor Barnes: *So, have you finished your research methodology?*

Student: *Not yet. I've decided to review my questionnaire design but I am a bit stuck with it.*

Professor Barnes: *Oh yes. How?*

Student: *Well, I just feel it's too open ended and I don't think I'll be able to categorize the answers. I'm not sure what I can do.*

Professor Barnes: *Have you thought about giving options?*

Student: *I have, but what options should I include?*

Professor Barnes: *Yes, it is always a difficult decision. Well first you need to …*

Exercise 2

67

Listen to the tutorial between Inghar and her tutor, Professor Jackson. The tutorial is shorter than normal, but Inghar has three things she needs to do following her tutorial. Listen and note down the three things Inghar needs to do.

1 _____

2 _____

3 _____

What is a seminar?

In the UK, a seminar is a small group of 10–20 students who discuss an academic topic with a seminar tutor. Seminars are usually held in small rooms and are often linked to the lecture subjects. They are a chance to discuss ideas and readings with other students as well as a subject expert. Seminars are an important part of university life and can help you to understand your lectures and support your understanding of a topic.

In a seminar you may discuss other theories, ideas or related topics to the lecture programme. They can sometimes start with a presentation of linked material (such as related theories or recommended reading) and often students in the group take turns to prepare and present this material.

There are some key points to remember about seminars.

Glossary

clarify
To clarify something means to make it easier to understand, usually by explaining it in more detail.

- Seminars are an excellent time to clarify anything that you did not understand in a lecture. Remember, this clarification refers to where ideas are vague or you need more information. Do not use this time to complete your notes because you missed parts of the lecture. You need to focus on the specific questions being examined in the seminar. After the seminar you may be able ask your seminar tutor about anything you missed in the lecture.

- You should try and actively participate in seminars. They are a time for discussion and your seminar tutor will expect you to speak. Try to make sure that you give your opinion on a subject and say why you think that. You can agree and disagree with other students or theories that you have read.

- Remember that in a seminar you are part of a group, so do not do all of the speaking, but share it with your fellow students and make sure you let the discussion move on (do not always bring the discussion back to what you need for your assignment for example).

- You can and should take notes in a seminar. You will hear lots of good ideas. You can ask for clarification or further information on these ideas if needed, but remember not to dominate the seminar with these types of questions if you know you can find the information out yourself after the seminar.

Tip ✓ Sometimes the terminology used to describe a seminar or tutorial may differ from university to university too. Always check your course handbook or ask if you are unsure.

Tip

Exercise 3

Look at the following sentences below and categorize them into the boxes.

Asking for clarification	
Asking for Repetition	
Agreeing	
Disagreeing	
Expressing hesitation	
Adding further information	
Moving on	
Giving an opinion	

a	What do you mean by …?	i	On that topic, we can also …
b	Another point about that is …	j	In relation to that we could look at …
c	I think …	k	What was the writer that talked about X called?
d	I'm not too sure …		
e	In my opinion …	l	Can you spell that?
f	Well, I think it's debatable …	m	No, I don't think that …
g	I completely agree that …	n	Shall we look at the next point?
h	Could you say that again?	o	I'm in two minds about …

Expressing hesitation can sometimes be a way to disagree with someone if you are expressing hesitation about the person who spoke before.

> **For example:** 'I think Steinman's theory is quite relevant for today's climate.' 'I'm in two minds about how relevant it is. I think we could apply it to the East, but not really to the West.'

Exercise 4

Listen to the following seminar excerpt which is on the theories of education and note any key points below.

> Functionalist Theory:
>
>
> Concept: Theorist:
>
>
> Relation to today?

Now, check the audio script. Do you think you have noted down the most important information and ideas?

The US and Australian university systems

The words and conventions for university systems are not the same. They change by university and by country. Usually, university systems are **broadly** similar within a country, but different countries can have very different ways of naming and doing things. It is always useful to familiarize yourself with the system you are working in. To do this, always read through information on the university website (often the international section of a university website will have valuable information for you), and read through your course handbook for further information. Remember, you can ask questions at the administrative (admin) office of the university and they will help you.

Tip ✓ Always read your course handbook to find out how your university will deliver your course. This will help you understand what is required of you in lectures, seminars and tutorials.

Lectures

Exercise 5
The university system in the USA

70

Listen to Kate describing the university system in the USA and note in the boxes how it is different to the UK.

	UK	USA
Tutorials	One-to-one or small group discussions	
Seminars	Large group discussions of topics relating to the lectures.	
Lectures	Large talks where the lecturer talks	
Other differences		

Exercise 6
The university system in Australia

71

Listen to Bob describing the university system in Australia and note in the boxes how it is different to the UK.

	UK	Australia
Tutorials	One-to-one or small group discussions	
Seminars	Large group discussions of topics relating to the lectures.	
Lectures	Large talks where the lecturer talks	
Other differences		

Exercise 7

In science subjects, there is another form of listening which is used. Listen to Polly speaking and note down the other form of listening and a definition for it.

72

Pronunciation: Revision

Improving your listening skills includes improving your understanding of how English is pronounced. You need to know specific aspects such as how accents affect intelligibility, how speakers use their voice to add meanings and how and why sounds change in rapid speech. Being able to do these things will help you become an accurate listener and reduce mishearing which can result in poor notes and understanding.

The main way to improve your understanding is to listen a lot, notice the features you have learned about in chapters 1–8 and practise.

 Exercise 8

Look at the list of pronunciation features covered in chapters 1–8 below and try to remember what each is about and why it is important when listening to lectures. Then complete the table.

	Topic	What is it?	Why is it important?
Chapter 1	Rhythm and stress timing		
Chapter 2	Pausing and chunking		
Chapter 3	Unstressed words		
Chapter 4	Connected speech (joining words, disappearing sounds, changing sounds)		
Chapter 5	Intonation and emphasis for opinion/ importance including modal verbs and negatives		
Chapter 6	Connected speech		
Chapter 7	Rising and falling intonation		
Chapter 8	Using context to help with pronunciation		

Now put the chapters in order of difficulty for you.

Which areas do you need to practise more to improve your listening skills?

Tip ✓ Chapter 10 gives you useful resources to practise your listening. Try to listen to a variety of different accents and areas to improve generally.

Tip

Language: Polite language in discussions

Glossary

polite
Someone who is polite has good manners and behaves in a way that is socially correct and not rude to other people.

Often in discussions, you will hear language which is polite but indirect. Usually English is constructed around the idea of being polite to people, and so sometimes the direct meaning of what a person is saying is unclear. You need to understand this behaviour and the meaning behind the indirect speech.

> **For example:**
>
> 'I would review your conclusion if I were you.' = 'Review your conclusion'

Look at the following samples of language and their direct meaning.

1   'This reading list is good, but it needs work .' = Improve your reading list. It is not good enough.

2   'I think your ideas might need further thought.' = Improve your analysis, examples, evidence of your ideas.

3   'Hmm, I'm not sure the current thinking agrees with you.' = Current thinking does not agree with you.

4   'I'm sorry but I don't see your point.' = I don't understand you/agree with you.

5   'I don't think this line of argument has much weight.' = That is a weak argument.

6   'Your referencing could do with another review.' = Review your referencing

7   'You might want to resubmit another draft before the deadline.' = Submit another draft before the deadline.

8   'I'd suggest reading the article on Multiple Intelligences when you have the opportunity. ' = Read the article as soon as you can.

Exercise 9

Listen to the conversation extracts A–C and note down what each student needs to do and where each discussion takes place.

The student in A needs to: _____

Situation: _____

The student in B needs to: _____

Situation: _____

Students in C needs to: _____

Situation: _____

Tip ✓ Try to use polite language yourself. Using polite language is a useful tool to persuade people to help you.

Remember

✓ Listening in seminars and tutorials is slightly different to listening to lectures.

✓ It is useful to identify your strong and weak areas in pronunciation to minimize misunderstanding.

✓ Polite language is often used in English. It is useful to understand the meaning behind polite language. You could even try to use it yourself.

✓ Sometimes there is different terminology used in different universities and different countries. Familiarize yourself with your university's terminology.

10 | Moving forward

Aims ✓ know your strengths and weaknesses
      ✓ make an improvement plan
      ✓ recognize speaker 'mistakes'
      ✓ test your pronunciation

Aims

? Quiz
Self-evaluation

Match the advice in 1–9 with the correct chapter.

1	Familiarize yourself with a range of accents from native and non-native speakers.	Chapter 1
2	Use abbreviations to help speed up your note taking.	Chapter 2
3	Knowing the purpose of a lecture will help you focus your listening.	Chapter 3
4	Using your notes can help you prepare for your assessments.	Chapter 4
5	Reading about the topic before is a good way to feel prepared for a lecture.	Chapter 5
6	Pay attention to word stress as lectures often use it to highlight important points.	Chapter 6
7	Evaluate opinions using B.A.R.R.I.E.R.S.	Chapter 7
8	Knowing the structure of a lecture will help you follow the content better.	Chapter 8
9	In tutorials and seminars lecturers often use polite language to analyse your work.	Chapter 9

What are my strengths and weaknesses?

Self-evaluation is an important part of learning and you should evaluate your lecture listening abilities in detail if you want to improve. Difficulties with listening to lectures are due to many reasons such as speed of speaking, background noise, content, lack of preparation, accent, unknown vocabulary and others. You should get to know your strengths and weaknesses during the chapters in this book in order to become more self-aware. This will help you to focus on areas you need to improve whilst giving you confidence from understanding your strengths.

Exercise 1

Listen to three students talk about their listening abilities and decide which student Jing, Albert or Susanna is most like you.

Now listen again and decide which tips in 1–9 in the Quiz would be helpful for each student.

Jing: _____

Albert: _____

Susanna: _____

Exercise 2

Read the list of listening skills below and decide how good you are at each skill. Circle a number on the scale where 1 = weakness and 5 = strength.

1	I completed most of the notes correctly in the authentic lectures sections in this book.	1 2 3 4 5
2	I have a good understanding of how lectures are organized.	1 2 3 4 5
3	I know how to prepare for lectures.	1 2 3 4 5
4	My ability to understand connected speech has improved by doing the exercises in this book.	1 2 3 4 5
5	I know what kind of notes to take in a lecture.	1 2 3 4 5
6	My note taking skills have improved by doing the exercises in this book.	1 2 3 4 5
7	I understand how lectures use intonation for emphasis and meaning.	1 2 3 4 5
8	I know what seminars and tutorials are.	1 2 3 4 5
9	I am confident of my ability to deal with unknown words or complex vocabulary in a lecture.	1 2 3 4 5
10	I know the importance of certain grammatical structures for understanding lectures.	1 2 3 4 5

Discussion

Now read the advice for statements 1–10 in Exercise 2.

1 If you did well in these exercises, well done, but remember that a university lecture will be much longer so you should now practise with longer lectures. You can find many lectures from universities all over the world on the internet so make sure you take advantage of these resources and practise as much as possible. See the authentic lecture chapters 1–5 in this book for some additional practice. Revision chapters: all authentic lecture chapters

2 Make sure you know what lecture structures are common in your subject area. See if your university department has lectures available online so you can familiarize yourself with the style before your course. Revision chapters: 3 and 5

3 Real-life preparation will involve finding books and journal articles from the library or VLE as well as allowing time for the reading. Revision chapters: 2

4 A low score here is not a problem, it means you need more practice. But make sure you do practise because it will make listening to lectures much easier. Set yourself some goals and make a plan to listen to lectures every day. Revision chapters: 9

5 If you gave yourself a low score here, repeat the authentic lectures sections in this book. Revision chapters: authentic lecture chapters

6 You should have improved your note-taking skills with the exercises. If not, repeat as many exercises as necessary. Revision chapters: 5 and 7

7 You may need more practice to fully understand this aspect of lecturers' speaking styles. Revision chapters: all pronunciation sections chapters 1–9

8 Make sure you are clear about the format and structure of seminars and tutorials, and how they are different from lectures. Try to find out how many lectures, seminars and tutorials you will have on your course by looking at the university website and/or information from your department. Revision chapters: 2 and 9

9   Usually technical or subject specific vocabulary is not too difficult to learn (especially if there is a direct translation into your first language). Idiomatic language may be more difficult so try to increase your conversational vocabulary as much as possible before you start your course. Revision chapters: 4

10 This is often more difficult than learning subject specific vocabulary. If you gave yourself a low score for this statement make sure you revise the grammatical structures in this book. Revision chapters: all language focus sections chapters 1–9

How should I continue to practise?

By working through chapters 1–9 of this book you have increased your knowledge of lectures, learned new listening skills and improved your abilities by practising with authentic lectures. However, it is important that you continue to practise your listening skills so you need to make a plan. First, you should revise your weak areas by repeating exercises or whole chapters of this book – see Exercise 3 below. Second, you should make an improvement plan to continue building up your listening skills – see Exercise 4.

Exercise 3

Using the self-evaluation and discussion in Exercise 2, make a list of chapters in this book that you need to revise and skills you still need to improve.

Chapters to revise: _____

Skills to improve: _____

Making an improvement plan

Now that you have completed this book and evaluated your listening strengths and weakness, you should make a continuing improvement plan.

Divide your plan into two sections: What to do before you start university and what to do during your university course.

Exercise 4

75

Read Steffan's plan, then listen and complete the gaps with what he plans to do.

	June	July	August	September
Lecture practice	Listen for 15 mins Take notes & ask 1 _____	Listen for 30 mins Take notes & check	Listen for 45 mins Take notes & check	Listen for 60 mins Take notes & check
Education Vocabulary	Record all vocab in lecture Make a list of 2 _____ and learn	Review words from June's lectures Make a list of new words from lectures	Review words from July's lectures Make a list of new words from lectures	Review words from August's lectures Make a list of new words from lectures
Grammar	Listen for hedging and opinion grammar	Listen for tenses and signposting	Listen for special phrases	Listen for 3 _____
Understanding accents	Try to hear the difference between USA & UK	Practise with others like 4 _____	Listen to Australian lecturers because the accent is difficult	Listen to many and decide which are difficult for me.

Exercise 5

76

Now listen to Dr Roke, an education lecturer, evaluate Steffan's plan and answer the following questions.

1   According to Dr Roke, what are the strengths of Steffan's plan?

_____

2   What does the teacher suggest Steffan should do to make his plan more effective?

_____

3   How does Steffan's plan relate to current theories on effective learning?

_____

4   What aspects of university listening might surprise Steffan, even after his preparation?

_____

5   What does Dr Roke recommend Steffan should do during his BA Education course?

_____

Exercise 6

Make a two-step improvement plan for you. Think about 4 areas to focus on in each month. Use the tables below.

Before my course				
Area of focus	June	July	August	September
1				
2				
3				
4				

During my course				
Area of focus	October	November	December	January
1				
2				
3				
4				
	February	March	April	May
1				
2				
3				
4				

- Improvement plan 1: before my course
- Improvement plan 2: during my course

Language: 'Mistakes' of the speaker

Native speakers are not 'perfect' speakers and this applies to lecturers too. Some people are what we call 'natural public speakers'. They seem confident and are often funny and dynamic when they lecture. Other lecturers can be shy or less confident and find the experience less rewarding than seminars or tutorials.

All lecturers, whether they are shy or confident, native speakers or non-native speakers make mistakes when they speak. This is because speaking is not planned in the same way as writing. Here are some common mistakes you might hear.

Wrong facts and figures: Large numbers, fractions, percentages, equations, quantities, dates, names etc. can easily be confused. Usually the lecturer will notice and self correct.

Grammar mistakes: These are usually small and happen because the speaker is processing complex information in the brain at the same time as speaking. The lecturer will usually notice and self correct.

Losing the thread of the argument: This can happen if the lecturer digresses from the main point, tells a story or anecdote or tries to simplify complex information. Suddenly s/he can no longer remember the main point and says something that is not logical or connected. Usually the lecturer will notice, apologize, pause, re-think what they wanted to say and repeat the information.

'Stumbles' over words: Sometimes the lecturer might make a mistake with a word or stutter when they start the word. This can often happen because lecturers are speaking quickly or are a little nervous. Usually they will repeat the word to correct it.

Exercise 7

Listen to the following six mistakes, highlight where the error is and categorize them according to the terms on page 135.

1 'So there are in fact six hundred thousand dollars in the budget for ... I mean six hundred million dollars ...'

2 'Nothing hasn't been added to this theory for years.'

3 'The key elements of learner aumoton ... autonomy...'

4 'So, after we look more deeply into this theory we can see that ... We can see ... That's the theory.'

5 'So, some prime examples of this kind of behaviour can be seen across the world. Particularly in the USA and Japanese.'

6 'So, this is quite prevalent in education. Next we're going to look at ... oh ... one minute ... I've lost my place. Aha here ... Montessori.'

Remember there are many ways that speakers show they have made mistakes or self-corrected. By regularly listening to people you will gradually become familiar with many of these ways and begin to use them yourself.

Pronunciation review

In chapters 1–9 you learned about speed, stress timing, pausing and chunking, unstressed words and connected speech, intonation, hesitation and false starts.

Exercise 8

Listen and write the exact words you hear. Then mark the features of pronunciation, for example intonation or connected speech. Listen as often as you want.

78

1 _____

2 _____

3 _____

4 _____

5 _____

6 _____

7 _____

8 _____

9 _____

10 _____

Evaluate your strengths and weaknesses for each aspect of pronunciation below. Write S (strength) or W (weakness) next to each one.

A I can hear word stress used to emphasize key points.

B I can hear word stress used to show contrast.

C I can hear meaning expressed through intonation.

D I can understand 'chunks' of language.

E I can recognize or 'guess' the grammar of unstressed words.

F I can understand fast speakers.

Remember

✓ Always prepare before a lecture

✓ Know the purpose of lectures

✓ Know the structure and organization of lectures

✓ Try to practise listening to real lectures as much as possible before you start university

✓ Practise different note-taking styles until you find one that suits you

✓ Know what notes you should take and why

✓ Always do something with your notes after each lecture

✓ Learn the techniques and strategies in this book to help you improve your listening

✓ Evaluate your strengths and weaknesses in listening to lectures

✓ Take responsibility for your own learning and make a plan to improve your weaknesses

LECTURE

5 | Learner autonomy

Preparation 1

You are going to listen to a lecture entitled 'Learner autonomy'. Before you listen, prepare for the lecture using some of the techniques outlined in this book. List the techniques you would like to use below.

> Technique 1: Understand the meaning of the title of the lecture, by looking up unknown words or doing an online search.
>
> Technique 2: Write down everything you know about the topic.
>
> Technique 3: _____
>
> Technique 4: _____
>
> Technique 5: _____

For more information on preparation techniques, see Chapter 2 and the preparation sections of Lectures 1–4.

Preparation 2

Now follow the techniques and write notes on what you learned.

Technique 1: Understand the meaning of the title of the lecture, by looking up unknown words or doing an online search.

_____

Technique 2: Write down everything you know about the topic.

_____

Technique 3: _____

_____

Technique 4: _____

_____

Technique 5: _____

_____

Preparation 3

You are going to listen to the final section of the lecture. Look at the handout of the lecture slides to familiarize yourself with their content.

Slide 12

> **LEARNING STYLES**
> - Many different labelling systems for example:
> - Honey & Mumford 1982
> - Kolb
> - Ellis & Sinclair 1989
> - Willing
> - Gardner

Slide 13

>
>
> **Howard Gardner**
> 1943–
>
> Professor of cognition and education Harvard Graduate School of Education
>
> - *Frames of Mind*
>
> The theory of multiple intelligences (MI)
> - Musical intelligence
> - Bodily-kinaesthetic intelligence
> - Logical-mathematical intelligence
> - Linguistic intelligence
> - Spatial intelligence
> - Interpersonal intelligence
> - Intrapersonal intelligence

Slide 14

Slide 15

Concluding thoughts

- Cooperation/collaboration
- Find techniques/learning styles
- Be self aware

Authentic lecture

> Lecture: Learner Autonomy
> Lecturer: Celia Wigley
> Accent: English

 Listen to the final section of the lecture and write your notes for each
slide. Remember that you are trying to note down the key points.

Writing up your notes

Once the lecture has finished, type your notes up so that you have a clear
record of the content of the lecture. Use your notes from the previous
exercise and type these up so that they are easy for you to refer to.

Reflection

✓ How much did the preparation help you with note taking?

✓ Did you find you could write quickly enough?

✓ Would you need to record this lecture and listen more than once?

✓ Compared your notes to the answer key.

✓ Do you have all the underlined main points as in the sample notes?

✓ Listen again and read the audio script.

✓ Are your notes accurate? Check the accuracy against the audio script.

✓ If you completed the notes and have the main points and have
represented the lecture accurately, well done!

✓ If you have incomplete notes, only some main points and have some
inaccuracies, use Chapter 10 to help you make a further study plan.

To listen to the complete lecture and read the full transcript of the lecture, visit www.collinselt.com/academicskills

Learner resources

There are many online resources to practise listening to academic lectures and features of spoken English. Here are some which you can use to continue practising and improving your skills.

Lectures

- www.TED.com

  This website has many lectures from leading academics all over the world. The talks are mostly short, come with video and the speakers have a wide range of accents.

- www.apple.com/education/itunes-u/

  Many universities from all over the world have lectures you can download from iTunes.

- http://www.bbc.co.uk/worldservice/learningenglish/general/talkaboutenglish/2009/04/090427_tae_al.shtml

  In this BBC series you can listen to students talking about listening to lectures and get advice on listening to lectures.

- http://bigthink.com/ and http://www.academicearth.org/

  These sites have lectures and talks from leading academics around the world on a range of topics.

- http://www.futurelearn.com/ and https://www.coursera.org/ and http://oli.cmu.edu/ and http://www.open.edu/openlearn/

  These are online education organizations providing free short courses from universities in the USA and Europe. They have many online lectures covering a variety of subjects.

- http://www.bbc.co.uk/podcasts/genre/learning

  The BBC has many podcasts which are semi academic and would be useful for listening practice.

Pronunciation

- http://www.bbc.co.uk/worldservice/learningenglish/grammar/pron/
  The BBC has a pronunciation section with exercises for practice.

- http://www.manythings.org/e/pronunciation.html
  There are pronunciation practice exercises here.

Glossary

Some of the more difficult words from the chapters are defined here in this Glossary. The definitions focus on the meanings of the words in the context in which they appear in the text. Definitions are from *COBUILD Advanced Dictionary*.

Key			
ADJ	adjective	PHRASAL VERB	phrasal verb
N-COUNT	count noun	PHRASE	phrase
N-UNCOUNT	uncount noun	VERB	verb
N-VAR	variable noun		

a

attention span (attention spans) N-COUNT
Your *attention span* is the amount of time that you can concentrate on a particular task, activity, or subject without becoming distracted.

c

chronological ADJ
If things are described or shown in chronological order, they are described or shown in the order in which they happened.

clarify (clarifies, clarifying, clarified) VERB
To clarify something means to make it easier to understand, usually by explaining it in more detail.

complex ADJ
Something that is complex has many different parts, and is therefore often difficult to understand.

concentrate (concentrates, concentrating, concentrated) VERB
If you concentrate on something you give all your attention to it.

consonant (consonants) N-COUNT
A consonant is a sound such as 'p', 'f', 'n', or 't' which you pronounce by stopping the air flowing freely through your mouth.

controversial ADJ
If you describe something or someone as controversial, you mean that they are the subject of intense public argument, disagreement, or disapproval.

critique (critiques) N-COUNT
A critique is a written examination and judgement of a situation or of a person's work or ideas.

d

digress (digresses, digressing, digressed) VERB
If you digress, you move away from the subject you are talking or writing about and talk or write about something different for a while.

discredit (discredits, discrediting, discredited) VERB
To discredit an idea or evidence means to make it appear false or not certain.

disprove (disproves, disproving, disproved, disproven) VERB
To disprove an idea, belief, or theory means to show that it is not true.

e

emphasis (emphases) N-VAR
Emphasis is special or extra importance that is given to an activity or to a part or aspect of something.

ensure (ensures, ensuring, ensured) VERB
To ensure something, or to ensure that something happens, means to make certain that something happens.

f

formulate (formulates, formulating, formulated) VERB
If you formulate a thought, opinion, or idea you express it or describe it using particular words.

g

go over PHRASAL VERB
If you go over your work, a situation, or a system, you consider it carefully to see what is wrong with it or how it could be improved.

i

ideology (ideologies) N-VAR
An ideology is a set of beliefs, especially the political beliefs on which people, parties, or countries base their actions.

intensive ADJ
Intensive activity involves concentrating a lot of effort or people on one particular task in order to try and achieve a great deal in a short time.

intonation (intonations) N-VAR
Your intonation is the way your voice rises and falls as you speak.

j

journal (journals) N-COUNT
A journal is a magazine that deals with a specialist subject.

l

literary ADJ
Literary means concerned with or connected with the writing, study, or appreciation of literature.

m

modify (modifies, modifying, modified) VERB
If you modify something, you change it slightly usually in order to improve it.

o

objective ADJ
If someone is objective, they base their opinions on facts rather than their personal feelings.

overview (overviews) N-COUNT
An overview of a situation is a general understanding or description of it as a whole.

p

polite (politer, politest) ADJ
Someone who is polite has good manners and behaves in a way that is socially correct and not rude to other people.

pose questions (poses, posing, posed) VERB
If you pose a question, you ask a question.

prejudice (prejudices) N-VAR
Prejudice is an unreasonable dislike of a particular group of people or things, or a preference for one group of people or things over another.

preparatory ADJ
Preparatory actions are done before doing something else as a form of preparation or as introduction.

process (processes) N-COUNT
A process is a series of actions carried out in order to achieve a particular result.

r

real time N-UNCOUNT
If something is done in real time, there is no noticeable delay between the action and its effect or consequence.

refer (refers, referring, referred) VERB
If a word refers to a particular thing, situation, or idea, it describes it in some way.

relate (relates, relating, related) VERB
If something relates to a particular subject, it concerns that subject.

rhythm (rhythms) N-VAR
A rhythm is a regular series of sounds or movements.

s

subjective ADJ
Something that is subjective is based on personal opinions and feelings rather than on facts.

subtitle (subtitles) N-COUNT
Subtitles are a printed translation of the words of a foreign film that are shown at the bottom of the picture.

symbol (symbols) N-COUNT
A symbol is something that represents or stands for something else.

t

terminology (terminologies) N-COUNT
The terminology of a subject is the set of special words and expressions used in connection with it.

v

vowel (vowels) N-COUNT
A vowel is a sound such as the ones represented in writing by the letters 'a', 'e', 'i', 'o', and 'u', which you pronounce with your mouth open, allowing the air to flow

Audio scripts

Audio scripts that appear in a box are authentic recordings.

Chapter 1 The purpose of lectures

Track 01

Extract 1
Good morning everyone, my name is Claire and I work for Student Services. Today I want to talk to you about your accommodation contract and what some of the legal terms mean. The university has a standard contract for all its residences and you need to know what your responsibilities are. So, in the next hour I'll be explaining all the key points.

Extract 2
So, in this session I will be explaining the various aspects of housing policy and how it relates to modern government policy. This is one of the biggest changes in recent decades. Does everyone have a handout? Good. Okay, so let's start by describing the origin of the policy ...

Extract 3

Henry	Hello. Can I help you?
Jing	I hope so. I'd like some information about places to live in the city.
Henry	OK, have you thought about which area of the city you'd like to live in and how much you'd like to spend per month?
Jing	A little bit, but I'd appreciate your advice.
Henry	Of course ...

Extract 4

Louise	Hello Lucy, how are you?
Lucy	I'm fine thanks, although there's so much to do before the holidays and I still haven't found a new house yet.
Louise	Why are you moving?
Lucy	Well, to be honest I'd like to live closer to the university, even if it is a bit more expensive.
Louise	You know, we've got a spare room in our flat and it's only 10 minutes' walk from the campus. Why don't you come round and see if you like it?
Lucy	That's a great idea, I'll come round later.

Track 02

Man	Well, I've been lecturing for about 40 years now, and it's changed a lot. I remember my first lecture; it was me, the board and about 100 students. It was a bit of a scary experience. I've seen lots of changes since then, mainly when screens were introduced. We started with overhead projectors, where I would project slides so that the students could see them, to PowerPoint presentations which everyone uses, and now finally to interactive

white boards. I'm a professor in philosophy, but sometimes I feel like a professor of technology!'

Woman   'I lecture in pharmacy at the local university. The lecture theatre has room for about 60 students. It's got a lectern at the front, but I don't like to use it. I always try to make the lecture interesting. I bring in handouts to help students make notes. There isn't time for discussion in the lectures, lectures are more like presentations, but students can always bring questions to their tutorials instead.'

Track 03

See sentences in Chapter 1.

Track 04

See sentences in Chapter 1, Exercise 5.

Track 05

So, how can we effectively negotiate? Well, <u>first of all</u> let me define negotiation. A common definition we could use is that it's any attempt to sway or influence someone else's decisions, thinking or actions. Now, people do this every day … <u>it can be seen</u> when children share toys, when people decide what they're going to eat in an evening, more seriously, between businesses and governments … but with varying degrees of success. Some people have a propensity for getting what they want, but others <u>end up</u> the loser in negotiation. <u>The key to great negotiation</u> is knowing what you want out of a negotiation, but then, not just making yourself heard, <u>the real winner in negotiation </u>is to listen to the other party. Make sure they feel like they're being heard. It must be remembered that negotiation is <u>a two-way street.</u> It is not the art of manipulation. Any great negotiator can understand <u>the implicit choices the other party is making</u>. We're going to look at these choices more explicitly over the next couple of weeks<u>, as well as </u>covering the negative elements of negotiation, but <u>let's look to</u> some examples of great negotiators and why they were so good. Let's start with Ghandi. Now, he needs no introduction as a person, but as a negotiator? Well, not only did Ghandi manage to <u>build up</u> massive support, he also negotiated change in his own way. A non-confrontational way. As many of the most successful negotiators do….

Chapter 2 Preparing for lectures

Track 06

Interviewer   Hi Sarah. I'm trying to find out some information about preparing for lectures to put in an advice booklet for new students. So could you give me some ideas?

Sarah   Of course. You know I used to worry about going to lecturers because I found it so difficult to concentrate for an hour when I first started university. But now I've got a set of preparation techniques which help me get the most of my lectures.

Interviewer   Great. Tell me, what do you do?

Sarah   Well, it's important that new students realize that they can't just go and speak to their lecturers before the lecture. Preparing for a lecture is really our responsibility as students. And there's no point reading too much otherwise you'll just get confused. So, really I'd recommend doing a little bit of reading in a general textbook, talking about the lecture with your friends and making a list of things you want to know from the lecture. Doing these things helps me to focus on the lecture but not get too stressed.

Interviewer   Those are great ideas, thanks.

Lectures

James   Students often get worried when they see unknown terminology on a lecture title and this makes them think that they won't understand the content of the lecture. This is often not true. What I would advise is looking up the meaning of unknown terminology – a dictionary of business terms or reference book is fine for this and then think about how much you understand it. Remember that a lecturer will usually give definitions and examples of new words and phrases and that we don't expect students to understand everything before the lecture. I really want to stress that reading a lot before a lecture is not necessarily a good idea.

Students should try to focus their reading as much as possible on the topic of the lecture – don't just read generally and try to develop a process for preparing for lectures. For example, if we take the title of one of my lectures, 'The impact of print, online and visual media on election results in EU countries post 2000' there are several things a student could do. First of all, if I were them, I would check the meanings of the key phrases here: media and what constitutes print, online and visual as the lecturer may have different definitions from those used in everyday language. Then I would go to the library and search out books with an introduction to media and elections – reading one or two chapters on each would be enough in my opinion. This simple three-step technique of checking key terms, finding introductory books to the topic and reading one or two focused chapters, could be used by students to prepare for any lecture really. The connection between the topics, the impact part, is the topic of my lecture – students don't need to know all that.

Track 08

Sarah   So, I don't really like going to lectures because I always come out thinking there's so much I don't know. But I try to prepare as much as possible beforehand – I hate it if I get lost or lose the thread of the topic. Some lecturers speed up when they get excited about something and that's when I start to lose focus. Anyway, I make sure I have a look at my notes from the last lecture to refresh my memory and see if there are any connections. Then I chat to my flatmates about it – we're all studying Economics so that's nice. Then I check the reading list and reserve any books online. It's always good to do that before the lecture – usually what happens is that students come out of the lecture and go straight to the library so I try to be one step ahead of everyone if possible! Then I like to have a quick flick through the books a couple of days before the lecture. Just to get an overview of the subject really.

Track 09

So, can everyone see the systems on this slide clearly? (2–3 sec pause) Is that better now? (2–3 sec pause) Okay, great. Now what I want to talk about here is how this first one is used by the government to predict the popularity levels of their policies in online surveys. This is a key issue for political parties and something that political analysts and bureaucrats have been struggling with for years. (2–3 sec pause) You see there is a trade-off between asking the questions and putting ideas into people's heads. What do you think this might be? (5 sec pause) Exactly, the positive results of one set of survey data may cause negative results in another set as each survey is sent to a specific target group. Surveys require specialist researchers to compile and analyse them which costs money; badly formed surveys usually produce data which is of little use to governments, right? (5 sec pause) So we are going to look at the construction of these surveys using this system and assess some previous results in terms of accuracy and reliability.

Track 10

As a result of studying urban behavior in large cities/ we are now just beginning to understand/the effects of new building schemes on creating harmony.

Track 11

See sentences in Chapter 2, Exercise 10.

Track 12

1 There are many functions of governments; overseeing economic growth and creating policy to name a few. In this lecture I'd like to draw your attention to their role in international relations. Often, a government's stance on foreign policy can have wide-reaching effects on all the roles a government plays.

2 So overall the ingredients to success in business are complex and industry dependent. As I've just said, there are some elements that all businesses need to survive, things like control over cash flow and of course, adequate business planning.

3 We're going to leave the pro-examinations sectors for now. Opposing this view are many educationalists in primary education. We can see this by looking at the strikes and petitions to governments by primary school teachers.

Authentic lecture 1: Bill Gates and philanthrocapitalism

Track 13

So you're still wondering, I'm sure, what is philanthrocapitalism? So first of all, let's look at philanthropy. So we know that philanthropy is the act of giving to, or doing something for poor people or those who need help, or giving to a— a good cause. A philanthrocapitalist is a business person, primarily, who believes that business should not just be about profit. But that business has a moral duty to give back to the society that gave it so much.

Philanthrocapitalists believe that they are better poised, through their extensive business skills and their background in business, to deliver philanthropy in a way that maybe will be more efficient or specific than government programmes alone. Gates r— regularly cites vaccines as one of the best forms of global investment and giving. So he sees this as— as offering up the best return, i.e. the best chance of saving lives, especially young lives, at the lowest cost. So as you see in that example, he applies business principles to his choices in philanthropy.

One of the most interesting things related to the Bill and Melinda Gates Foundation, is the Giving Pledge. So this is something that Bill Gates and legendary financier Warren Buffett formed in 2010. And the Giving Pledge works like this. Basically, they focus on billionaires ... um ... excuse me ... they get them to agree to give away at least half of their wealth to philanthropic causes within their lifetimes or after their deaths. Um, now th— this pledge is— is really just a verbal promise. They don't sign a contract. And they do, however, make a very public commitment to give away the majority of their fortunes. So for example on their website, they have a long list of ... um ... the people who have agreed to this pledge. It includes names like Mark Zuckerberg of Facebook and a brief explanation from each person who's sign— who has ... um ... not signed on, but agreed to this pledge. Gives an explanation of why they've chosen to do that. So far, they have managed to sign up just under one hundred American billionaires, which is quite amazing when you think about the fact that it's only been going on since 2010. And now they're starting to focus on China and other countries where there's a lot of wealth being generated.

Chapter 3 The structure of lectures

Track 14

1 At some point, we'll look at the effects of deforestation …

2 So, we've covered the effects of deforestation …

3 We've started out with the effects of deforestation …

4 I'd like to turn to the effects of deforestation …

5 We'll talk about the effects of deforestation in a little while …

6 Now, onto the effects of deforestation …

7 I've talked a bit about the effects of deforestation …

8 We're going to come back to the effects of deforestation …

9 So, that's the effects of deforestation …

10 At some point we'll go over the effects of deforestation …

Track 15

1 Morning everyone. I'd like to start today's session by outlining what I want to cover. Essentially I'll be talking about Kepler's three laws of planetary motion and their importance in modern cosmology. I'm going to talk about each law in quite a lot of detail so you can develop your understanding of each one but I'm not going to include any historical background as we don't have enough time for that.

2 Right, let's get started, shall we? Current conservation projects are a focus of much environmental science research at the moment, especially in terms of their efficacy and long term effects and this is going to be the main theme of this lecture. What I want to do is look at the drivers behind these projects, who sets them up and why, by that I mean how is the need identified and how is the research conducted. Then we'll look at the changes these projects have recommended or produced and whether or not they were successful.

Track 16

Anterior surface

Constricted pupil

Pupillary ruff

Contraction furrows

Collarette

Crypts of Fuchs

Track 17

Okay? So this is just a schematic showing that. So the colour of our eyes is very individual. There's no two eyes the same. Even in i— you know – identical twins there may be some differences. Even though they are very genetically diff— … uh … s— similar, there may be some differences in how their— their irises look. And so this colour is very much dependent upon the pigmentation, or the melanin, that is contained on the anterior surface. So the front surface of the iris, as you can see as you're looking at it there.

Um, it's also thought that the colour of the eye is also ... um ... gen— it's sort of affected by the reflection and the absorption of certain wavelengths, long and ... um ... short wavelengths. So it's thought that in blue eyes, for example, there may be some changes in absorption and reflection of ... um ... certain wavelengths of light. That's not such a— an issue in brown eyes— in dark eyes, but maybe in blue it is. And possibly in some pale green eyes.

But essentially, if you look at the anterior surface we have, I'll just run through these and we'll go through them in a little bit more detail. This is a constricted pupil. We have this item called the pupillary ruff which is essentially— is like a pigmented ring which is on the inside of the iris and forms th— the margin of the pupil. And this essentially is the pigmented epithelium, which is showing through from the back of the iris. We have some of these sort of radial furrows, called contraction furrows and I'll talk about these in a second. We have a tissue here called the collarette, which basically does what it says on the packet, it looks like a collar. And that's actually the most— the thickest part of the iris. And then we have these structures called Crypts of Fuchs and again, I'll talk about these in a second.

Track 18

Conclusion 1

And there we are. Time's nearly up, so let's just recap what we've looked at. Firstly, global warming and where it's going, and more importantly how we can slow its progress. Alternative energy is one answer to this and although not in itself a panacea, we've looked at the need for development and research of alternative energy in particular, solar, wind, water, geothermal energy, and biofuels. The practicalities can hold back such energies as solar and wind. But nuclear energy may pave the way forward as I mentioned. Hollister talks about this in his book 'Nuclear Positive' which I'd recommend. But that's all for now. Enjoy your lunch and see you on Monday.

Conclusion 2

So, as you can see. Getting to where we are with the planets was a long process of discovery and although this solar system may be planetarily 'sewn up' so to speak, the discovery of solar systems outside our own is only beginning. Will we one day find another planet like our own? Imagine that. Do you think we'll even find something like that in your lifetime? Probably not in mine, but yours ... who knows? So, if you want to find out more about these developments, Smith and Bronte give a pretty thorough overview and that's on your reading list.

Conclusion 3

So, I think to conclude we can say that although exploration may be seen as a good thing, it can have disastrous effects when it comes to the sea bed, and the delicate eco systems there. So, I'd like you to think about this question. When exploration and further knowledge impacts upon ethics, where should we go? What can we do? Scientific ethics is part of this module and I'd like you to review the work we've done and come up with some ideas on positions we should take. There are no right answers, but it's certainly something we as scientists, and potential scientists, should be considering ...

Track 19
See sentence in Chapter 3, Exercise 10.

Track 20
1 It's been claimed that geologists will have clearly mapped most of the fault lines in California.

2 It's claimed that geologists haven't clearly mapped all of the fault lines in California.

3 It was claimed that geologists have clearly mapped none of the fault lines in California.

4 It was claimed that geologists had clearly mapped one of the fault lines in California.

Chapter 4 Features of speech

Track 21

Speaker 1	If everyone can take a look at the graph here, you'll see how the curve moves in a gradual gradient and if we change the data by 0.1% the difference is actually quite dramatic.
Speaker 2	The view through the microscope gives us a clear picture of the bacteria and we can now start to see it multiplying. Can you see? This will continue to happen as long as the bacteria are in the liquid.
Speaker 3	Robots are becoming increasingly common in all forms of manufacturing, although we have yet to see them being applied to domestic usages as much. Perhaps this will be the next wave of robotics developments.
Speaker 4	Since the turn of the 21st Century chemists have thought that there must be further elements to the periodic table and that they would be found given enough time and research.

Track 22

Extract 1

So, it <u>turns out</u> that this is a really complex problem and students often <u>run into</u> difficulties in their experiments because they think the solution <u>has got something to do with</u> cell structure.

Extract 2

So, to summarize, the effects of radiation on the human body are directly related to the amount of exposure to the sources.

Extract 3

We've had a lot of examples of acid deposits here, which we've been able to identify as industrial chemicals released into the river.

Extract 4

Now, let's look at the cell in the diagram more closely these cells will burst when immersed in pure water which is actually quite weird to watch under a microscope.

Track 23

Well, the field of automation is one of the quite controversial areas of AI. Now, automation has great effects on levels of productivity, but some commentators claim that this area is now a greater threat to job security than outsourcing. It may seem drastic, but think of examples in our own lives; how many people here use ATMs instead of going to the bank clerk, or use a self-checkout in a supermarket instead of going to the till operator?

Track 24

See words in Chapter 4, Exercise 4.

Track 25

See words in Chapter 4, Exercise 5.

Track 26

See sentence in Chapter 4.

Track 27

See sentence in Chapter 4.

Track 28

See sentence in Chapter 4.

Track 29

1 Today's lecture is going to touch on some of the key theories of game theory.

2 So, you can see that this experiment hasn't provided much useful data.

3 Astronomers have tried to discover what the exact function of Saturn's rings are.

4 The soil in this region is so porous that it is unlikely that any plants will be able to get their roots to take hold.

Track 30

Lecturer 1	It is still unclear exactly how current technological advances will affect our everyday lives but it is likely that changes will occur in three broad areas, biotechnology, governance and employment. It can be argued that other areas will be affected too, however, they are outside the scope of this lecture.
Lecturer 2	Okay everyone, let's start with a question. It is still unclear exactly how current technological advances will affect our everyday lives but it is likely that changes will occur in three broad areas. Can you discuss what you think they might be? [pause] Well, they are biotechnology, governance and employment. It can be argued that other areas will be affected too, however, they are not what we are going to be discussing today.
Lecturer 3	So, it is still kind of unclear exactly how current technological advances will affect everyone's everyday lives you know, but it is fairly likely that changes are gonna occur in three broad areas, and these are 1. biotechnology, 2. governance and 3. employment. Some academics argue that other areas will be affected too, however, we're not going to bother with those today.

Track 31

Right, now let's move onto examining the flora and fauna of the Kalahari Desert. After the drainage of the lake over 10,000 years ago the area became more arid however it is not technically a desert. Why? Well, mainly because of the annual rainfall which exceeds three inches in most years. During the rains the region is a haven for various forms of wildlife – here you can see animals grazing. But what I want us to focus on is the abundant vegetation instead. Even though the area appears arid and desolate, surprisingly there are countless species both native and introduced. Many of these plants are fundamental to maintaining the delicate balance of the ecosystem and in terms of environmental science we are beginning to realize their importance in regulating herd size in the Kalahari.

Authentic lecture 2: A brief overview of tsunamis

Part 1: Track 32

Okay good morning everyone. Today we're going to be talking about tsunamis. And what I'd like to do today is to give you a brief overview of some of the mechanics of tsunamis and their context and how they are propagated. Uh, first of all, what is a tsunami? Now a tsunami is any sudden non-meteorological induced impulse in the water, regardless of size. And this is a definition from Landers et al. 'The Science of Tsunami Hazards'.

Now on the left of this slide, I've shown two of the characters for tsunamis from the Japanese. Now, tsunamis often travel at very great speed and with a sufficient force to inundate the land. Frequently, they're named—they're misnamed 'tidal waves'. Now, the Japanese use this term in the context that destructive waves often develop resonant phenomenon. So in the 1700s and the 1800s they noticed this phenomena, and sometimes before that, where they saw these harbour or port-crossing, which is the word 'Tsu' in Japanese, and 'Nami', wave. And that often these harbour or port crossing waves were associated with a lot of destruction, so they were named Tsunamis. So there's a great history of tsunamis in the literature.

Now there are three main aspects of tsunamis that I'd like to talk about today. The first is going to be the generation of tsunamis. The second, the propagation and the third, the landfall of them. We'll look at each one of these, in part, in this lecture.

Part 2: Track 33 (Slide 2.1)

Now, we've talked a bit about the generation of the tsunami. So we've started out with the earthquake. The earthquake has occurred, the earthquake generates energy, this energy is transmitted to the bottom of the ocean floor. This is then transmitted to the whole water column. Now imagine with the water column. How deep is the water column? So in the deep ocean, we're talking about water that might be ten, fifteen kilometres deep. And this we're now going to look at. So we have this energy. It's been transmitted into this water column. And right now, I'm showing you an overview of—where we have the motion of the fault-block and then the tsunami originated. And we're in the deep water right now. Later on, we'll talk about the shallow water and how this is transmitted to land.

For this next part, we want to talk about what happens in the ocean itself. Because we have the energy that has been transmitted and it's going from the bottom of the ocean to the top of the ocean. And the energy's going to stay in this water column, but the way it manifests itself is going to be waves at the top of the ocean. So now we have energy in the whole water column and it is being transmitted to the top of the ocean.

(Slide 2.2)

So now we need to go back and think about what is the depth of the deep ocean. And I made a mistake before, which often happens when we're lecturing, and I told you that the ocean's depth was 20 to 30 kilometres. In fact, and I'm glad one of you noticed because I saw your hand up, the water depth is actually, in the deep ocean, two to four kilometres.

Now this is slightly confusing but we have a mathematical theory called Deep Water Theory. And Deep Water Theory is quite complicated. It only applies if the water depth is greater than the wave length divided by two. So what did we say the wave length divided by two was? We said it was 25 to 150 kilometres for a typical tsunami. But this isn't true for the deep ocean. The deep ocean, we have two to four kilometres. So that means we know the Deep Water Theory is not going to apply in the deep ocean. Now Shallow Water Theory, in mathematical theory, is where the depth is less than the wave length divided by twenty. Now let's take 25 to 150 kilometres. Let's divide that by twenty and we now have ten kilometres to s—... uh ... twenty kilometres. A little bit more.

And so what we have here is that the waves in the deep water, for a tsunami, follow Shallow Water Theory. Shallow Water Theory on a mathematics perspective, and I'll show this in the next slide, is much easier in terms of the equations so we're going to be using this. So the basic thing to take away from this is tsunamis follow shallow water theory in the deep ocean, as the depth a couple kilometres is much less than the wave wavelength, hundreds of kilometres.

(Slide 2.3)
Now this will be the only equation I'm going to show you in this lecture and it's one I'd like you to remember for the exam. The celerity of the waves, and celerity is another word for the speed or the velocity of the waves themselves, is equal to gravity times the depth of the ocean and then take that quantity and take the square root of it.

So what is gravity? Gravity in general is about ten metres per second squared. The depth we've been talking about—so let's take the depth at the deepest part of the ocean and let's say that's about four kilometres or 4000 metres. So if we have gravity ten metres per second squared, multiplied by depth of 4000 metres and then take the square root of that, that works out to a speed of about 200 metres per second. Or, if we could change this to kilometres per hour, about seven hundred kilometres per hour.

Now, through this a—very simple equation which has just two variables, and is pretty easy to manipulate, we now have an idea of how fast the waves are moving. So we have the earthquake, we have the generation through the water column, this produces waves at the top of the water column. And these waves are tens—tens of centimetres, and the speed of them in the deep ocean is around 700 kilometres per hour. So imagine the speed of a jet plane. So imagine that you're travelling from the United States to say, Africa, and it's going very quickly. That's about the speed in the deep ocean that the tsunami will be travelling.

Chapter 5 Understanding points

Track 34
See text in Chapter 5, Exercise 2.

Track 35
See text in Chapter 5, Exercise 3.

Track 36

Extract 1
So, there are a few forms of company structure which we are going to look at today. The first step on the business ladder, so to speak, is being a sole trader or partnership – this is where one or two people work in a business, but importantly they aren't a company – they're liable for their own losses. Then there are limited liability companies. This is quite common – these can be public or private and lastly, we've got co-operatives, which we'll talk more about in the next session as they can be quite complex.

Extract 2
Now let's turn to another relatively new phenomenon in marketing – and that's viral marketing – the marketer's dream! We're actually going to look at the three principles that marketers use for this to target the right customers effectively. The first thing is to gather social profiles. This gives marketing agencies

information on the right type of customer, so that they aren't for example selling ipads to 70 year olds but rather to the young people who have disposable income! Next they look at proximity marketing – which is looking at activities that person is already involved in online. This can tell you a lot about your potential customers and who should be your potential customers. Key word analysis is the last one. Researching real time key word density tells you what people are typing about – how common words or phrases are or might appear… let's explore these a little further.

Track 37

Extract 1
The fundamental principles of risk intelligence are all in some way related to transparency and defining roles, responsibility and authority within the organization.

Extract 2
Economists have all evaluated the role of the state differently and with good reason as far as I'm concerned. Their views have always been rooted in the socio-political events of the time which I firmly believe to be the right approach despite the theories of thinkers such as Keynes which attempt to be universally applicable.

Extract 3
Intellectual property or IP as it is known is one of the most complex areas of modern businesses both legally and in terms of business development as has been shown by Bloom and Davis. Their statistics demonstrate the potential value and therefore the risks of unprotected IP.

Track 38
There is even one idea on trade incentives which suggests increasing export tax will have a beneficial effect on company growth.

Track 39
See sentences in Chapter 5.

Track 40
See sentences in Chapter 5, Exercise 9.

Track 41
See sentences in Chapter 5, Exercise 10.

Track 42
1 We are currently focusing on the principles of accounting and we'll continue this for another three lectures. After that we're going to start looking at how these principles actually work in practice.

2 So let's look at the next slide showing the SWOT analysis of Nike. It's really easy to see how the online threats manifest themselves just by doing a simple Google search. You can also see the impact of online retail simply by the lack of new flagship stores in certain markets.

3 So has everyone read the report on the impact of sustainability policies on what we call the Big Four accounting firms? Now I want you to analyse the conclusions and recommendations that we made in light of the theories we covered last week.

Chapter 6 Thinking critically

Track 43
See sentences in Chapter 6, Exercise 3.

Track 44
At a recent town meeting, Dr David Burns identified two areas of economic growth in the town of Mullberry. Because the supermarket in town makes lots of money, Burn suggests the town should create more supermarkets therefore generating more money for the town. The other area that could be expanded is the pharmaceutical company that Dr Burns works within. As demand for medicines produced there is at a constant, and it offers jobs to many people, expanding this will mean more jobs and therefore more town income.

Track 45

Extract 1
So, now let's turn to Parnell's theory of social networking patterns. Although this really is groundbreaking research, as much study is when related to social networking the theory is essentially lacking. I think we'd have to call into question his research methods. If we look in depth at his study, the actual samples used were too small to extract any meaningful conclusions. This is why his theory is in dispute at the moment …

Extract 2
David Pollack has identified five areas to business success. These areas are quite interesting and his ideas are certainly sensible. Pollack has been quite accurate and measured in his assessment of necessities within business, and we can see a lot of agreement in practice for his identified areas.

Track 46
See sentences in Chapter 6.

Track 47
See sentences in Chapter 6, Exercise 10.

Track 48
See sentences in Chapter 6.

Track 49
See sentences in Chapter 6, Exercise 11.

Authentic lecture 3: The pursuit of innovation

Track 50

What does this mean for individuals? So we've talked a little about organizations, but what about individuals in this process? It's really hard to be an individual working in a large organization, whose responsibility it is to go out and get external ideas. It's a real hard graft of an activity. Many of your colleagues don't like external ideas. They're not well aligned to the corporate pro— processes and procedures, and they may not line up with your skills and capabilities that you're holding inside. They maybe take a while to exploit. You've got all these … uh … facilities that you've developed, brands that you've invested in. The last thing you want to do is someone to throw you a really radical idea, right? It can be very costly to implement that. So many organizations turn away from these external ideas.

But of course now, people are being pushed out into the world to hunt for external ideas. To go to places like Imperial College and find relationships with people here that may allow them to explore the merits. This is very challenging for many organizations— many individuals who work in the kind of traditional R and D environment. They have to manage a kind of new fluid model. So these are people who are really skilled in the arts of openness. People who know how to work with external parties, who know how to build relationships …uh… an— and successfully. So know how to talk the language of intellectual property, know when to approach an individual about a non-disclosure agreement. These are all skills that individuals have to acquire.

Right, the traditional R and D lab did not require this of many individuals. They worked for this hunt for 'new nylons', the internal process of discovery. They rely on internal knowledge, now they have to look externally for some of these ideas. In our own research, we've tried to look at the different role that individuals play in this process. And we've looked at … uh … a large organization and the role of different R and D staff in bringing in knowledge into the fray. And what we've found, is there are basically three roles that individuals take up in this process. Some individuals are explorers: they're out there hunting for exciting, new ideas. They're actively searching and scanning the external environment. Some people are really good at the assimilation process. They can take external ideas and make it— give it a local feel. Bring it in to the organization, and enthuse and engage their peers about these ideas and start to get them to take it up, to fit the categories of the firm. And then finally there is those people who just are very good at selling external ideas internally. They are passionate champions of these ideas. They take risks to overcome resistance within the organization of these external ideas. And of course there are some individuals who take on all three roles. And there are some take on none of these roles, who just look internally. What we found in our own research is that the individuals who take on all three roles have the highest individual performance. Those who can do all three stages of this process are the individuals who are really the— the people who are very best at doing work with innovation.

So it's not enough to just go out there and explore the external space. You need to think about how your idea is going to be assimilated internally. And how it's going to be championed and driven through into execution inside the organization. So you— when you're talking to— … uh … let's say you're an academic and you're talking to someone from the industry. You know, are they the explorers, are they assimilators or are they exploiters? Who is it you're talking to in the industry? Does the person you're talking to have the capacity to take your idea, transform it into an idea which is usable within the firm and eventually exploitable by that firm. Right? This is going to— this is going to affect the value of your relationship with that individual.

Chapter 7 Strategies for note taking

Track 51

Diane Foster   I spend most of my time researching and writing papers on research methodology skills, you know, things like how to match students' learning styles with types of academic research, mainly to help them choose a research project which matches their learning personality. For me note taking is an interesting area especially now that lecture recordings are widely available online. Actually, note taking is still extremely popular as many students find it helps to actually process the lecture content better. There are 4 main approaches and each has advantages and disadvantages. So, the List system is good because it's simple and students can choose how much to write but the biggest problem is that it doesn't really show how ideas relate to each other. This is much easier to do with the Mapping and Outline methods as they use colour coding and arrows or line. This makes it easier for students to re-read and understand their notes after the lecture. Mapping doesn't work for everyone though, especially more logical thinkers. Similarly, the outline method only works for students with good listening skills who can organize points well. It's a difficult method to use if the lecturer speaks fast or delivers content in a random way because your notes can end up looking like the list method instead. The Cornell method is often cited as the best note taking method because it is freer and forces students to review their notes and make sense of them by asking and answering questions. However, in my experience the main problem is that is only works with organized students who actually remember to follow the system. For less organized students I'd recommend using something different. Can I just finish up by saying that the most important point is to find a system that you like and that helps you make the most of your lectures.

Track 52

Dr Spenser   Right, everyone, are you ready? So, this morning I'm going to be giving you a brief background on Twain's early life and then focus the majority of the session on his literary influences and main works. So, Twain was the youngest of six children and grew up in Missouri. He was a bit of a troublemaker and left school, which he hated, at 12 after his father died. He had a series of jobs, firstly as an apprentice in a printer's shop and then at the Hannibal Journal where he became sub-editor and focused on the frontier style humour of satire and jokes that was popular at the time. He left his home in 1853 and became a bit of a wandering journalist before giving this up to work as a river pilot aged 24. He enjoyed this job – it was well paid and gave him a pretty good lifestyle but was forced to give it up by the start of the civil war in 1861. He enlisted and then deserted the military, went West to seek his fortune, failed and then started to write. It wasn't until after the civil war that became well known as an author rather than a journalist. Okay, so I'll leave it there. Although Twain has an interesting life, we really need to focus on his actual work so you'll have to research his life yourselves if you're interested.

In terms of his influences we can see some common themes in his works which we will be exploring in more depth throughout this semester. Right, so, first of all, there's the town of Hannibal where Twain grew up which was rooted in Southern traditions and the frontier lifestyle, including slavery. This particularly influenced *The Adventures of Tom Sawyer and Huckleberry Finn*. Aspects of the way of life in the American south such as the plight of slaves and financial hardship are present in Twain's fiction. Twain was also a prolific reader of classical writers such as Pliny as well as having an interest in the natural world and we can see evidence of both of these in his writing. Okay, so, let's take these three areas in more detail …

Track 53
See text in Chapter 7, Exercise 7.

Track 54

Lina   The thing I do in lectures is focus on the ideas I understand and write these clearly. I write down names, dates and numbers and key terms or vocabulary from the slides because my lecturer has used these as examples so I want to read about them afterwards. I also, try to listen to the end of a point and then write down some key words or phrases – and I might add some notes in my own language, German, if I can translate it quickly in my head.

Gregor   For me, the best way to take notes in lectures is to use mapping and lists. I use lots of colours and link up connecting ideas with the same colour arrows and lines. I try not to write too much because it's important to listen and understand the lecturers – but I always write down the examples as they are really useful for me.

Ozan   I like to write as much as possible in a free style and then rewrite my notes after the lecture. I'm not good at organizing and writing clearly during the lecture so I focus on quantity! Then I try to reduce my notes to the main points with clear examples and connections afterwards. My friends think it's too much work but it works for me!

Lectures

Extract 1
In terms of the Enlightenment there are three key areas: reason, the self and society. It emerged from a time of great social change in areas of economic prosperity, expansion of trade and empire, the industrial revolution and the development of diplomacy and legal systems. The prominent writers and thinkers of the time included Voltaire, Rousseau, Smith and Kant.

Extract 2
What we see when we look at employment law is that much of it is open to interpretation and although there are some areas which are standard such as sick pay, gross misconduct and maternity leave, other areas such as holiday allowance, access to training and childcare provision are very much up to the discretion of the employer. These grey areas are more often than not sources of conflict between employers and employees and need careful handling by solicitors. If we look at Cooke versus Leyton we can see a good example of what I mean.

Extract 3
As Pritchard notes sociolinguistics and psycholinguistics are connected through language. Therefore we will be studying the nature of language first covering systems of grammar and words both in written and spoken language. We will be comparing these systems across language families before we start to look at some of the key sociolinguistic questions such as the influence of language upon culture and vice versa. Then we'll consider some of the issues of psycholinguistics including where language is produced in the brain and how language is acquired.

Track 56
1 Brown's theory was quite controversial for its time, which is the reason for so many studies in this area.

2 We're going to look at the ideas that were developed in the late 1970s.

3 The Greeks were the main group who (that) contributed to the development of rational thought.

4 There are many aspects of company law but today we are going to focus on shares, which are actually quite an interesting area as you'll see later on.

Track 57
1 Although we can see many positives in Larson's study of the possible effects of improved urban living spaces, we still need to address more of the negatives such as cost and infrastructure.

2 I want to cover a range of topics in today's lecture including population density, income levels per capita, provision of facilities, governance, community.

3 So, what can the ancient world tell us about modern society? Are there lessons which we have learned from the writings of the great Greek thinkers. Well, despite what you might think, the answer to both these questions is yes.

Chapter 8 Understanding your notes

Track 58
Dr. Robinson Taking good notes can really make a difference when it comes to doing your assessments because your notes help you know what knowledge and ideas you know already and what you don't. So, therefore, this means you can plan your research and reading

time better. And also work out how long it's likely to take to do the actual assessment, whether it's an essay or report or presentation or whatever. If we look at Jamal's notes we can see that he's got quite a lot of good information down – general ideas, examples, details etc. but if he leaves his notes like this he's going to come across a few problems later on. Firstly, he should fill in some of basic details such as the other Nobel prize writers. And he needs to clarify anything that might be ambiguous. Here for example where it says 'Trans BUT also …'. Jamal might struggle to remember what that means if he doesn't clarify the meaning and add content pretty soon after the lecture. You see if Jamal doesn't fill in more details, he won't be able to work out which sections of his notes are relevant for his assessment. And he definitely needs to find out what those books and chapters are as soon as possible. Otherwise he could spend ages in the library or online trying to find them and if he doesn't know what chapters to read as follow up to the lecture, he could end up reading far too much unnecessary stuff and slowing down his progress.

Track 59

Sandra	So, Maria I think we need to work on your organization skills don't you?
Maria	Yes, I think so. It's definitely my weak point.
Sandra	Ok, let's start with your filing system on your laptop. Can I see what it looks like at the moment?
Maria	Here. It's not really organized properly – I know I need to sort it out.
Sandra	Right, mmm. So, what are you planning to do to organize it more logically?
Maria	Well, first of all, I need to label the folders better – by module and title and not by lecturer or just title. Our lecturers teach on more than one module so that's not a good way of labelling things. I'll definitely confuse myself if I carry on like that!
Sandra	Yes, I agree. And don't forget to categorize them by semester as well.
Maria	Oh yes, good idea.
Sandra	And what about these documents down here. All these need to go into folders and you need a better naming system too.
Maria	What about naming each one with the lecture title and the date?
Sandra	Much better. You might want to think about adding the name of the lecturer too.
Maria	Okay I will, thanks for your help Sandra.

Track 60

Professor Leslie	Let's now move on to the main thinkers behind the ideas of democracy. We'll start with a brief overview and then examine the texts in more detail. So, in Ancient Rome there are two main thinkers, Plato and Aristotle. Plato's work is from the 4th century BC and he describes how citizens of a country should think about their role in society. His ideas are about how people can understand their role in society by thinking about their abilities not how much money they have. Aristotle in the 3rd century BC talks about how the majority i.e. the voice of the people is most important. He also said that democracy is the least dangerous form of government. Now we'll look at these ideas in more detail later on.

Let's move on to the democracy in the UK. The first key event is the Magna Carta written in 1215. This document stated for the first time that the government must obey the law. The important thinkers were Hobbes in the 16th century and Locke in the 17th and Wollstonecraft in the 18th. Hobbes suggested that democracy would not work and claimed that power should be with the monarch, in other words the King or Queen should have total control. In contrast Locke spoke about the need for a contract between the government and the people – the government should protect the people and then they, the people, have the right to change the government if they don't keep to the contract. We'll also be considering the ideas of Mary Wollstonecraft here. She thought that people were equal including women and didn't believe in marriage.

So, finally we'll be looking at the French philosophers Montesquieu, Voltaire and Rousseau. The first two were doing their work in the 17th century and the last in the 18th. Montesquieu thought the monarchy should be limited and that various government powers should be separated. His ideas became the foundations for the constitution of the United States. That'll be in lecture 5 by the way. He also hated religion and didn't think it was good for society. Voltaire believed in the importance of reason as he thought it lead to social progress. His view was that government is good if people are protected by laws and democracy works only if countries aren't large. Finally, we have Rousseau. He believed that the rule of law belonged to the people not the government and that people should rise up and change the government if it does nothing to represent their beliefs. His views formed the basis of the French Revolution. Okay, so …

Track 61

1 The age of Romanticism is fascinating in terms of how it changed the way in which people in general interacted with works of fiction.

2 When we think about the purpose of art galleries it is clear that they play a key public role in national culture.

3 Bartlett's study of inner city housing concludes that the role of poverty should be studied far more in future.

4 Right so if everyone looks at the slide here, which is an analysis of the text, we can see some interesting features.

5 Let's now turn to the thinking of Plato where we can see how he outlines his ideas on democracy.

Track 62

See text in Chapter 8, Exercise 9.

Track 63

When we try to look for connections or cause and effects in archaeological research we are trying to see where logical connections are. Let's say we want to know where a piece of pottery or glass is from, first we need to analyse the soil and see if there is a match on our database. If we can't find anything we'll look at the material of the pottery or glass itself and see if we have other samples which are the same so we can compare them.

Authentic lecture 4: The history of universities in Western Europe

Part 1: Track 64

I'd like to turn to thinking about, broadly, how … uh … the modern university emerged. And I'm going to go right the way back to the classical inheritance of Greco-Rome education— Greco-Roman education, sorry. Now … um … classical learning was incredibly sophisticated. And … um … there were many schools which … uh … were available to … uh … men, obviously, but a wide range of men in the empire. In 70 AD, the Emperor Vespasian even established some professorships— some chairs, of Geek and Latin, because he recognized the importance of a well-educated population to the administration of the empire.

Now I bring this up because the way that learning was done in the classical world, through a process of dialectic, is still really important in the way that we create knowledge today. Dialectic, quite a tricky word. Um, dialectic basically means establishing something as correct, or true, through a dialogue between people who hold different opinions on it. So they are using reasoning to try and establish the— the truth on a subject.

Some of these subjects continue to have resonance, even in the modern day, which started off as classical debates. Um, a famous one, which … uh … links classical thinkers with modern philosophers, is the nature of universals. By universals, I mean things like … uh … is goodness something you can only see in individual acts of being good? Or is goodness something that exists in the abstract? Can we decide that something is good or bad without having an example of it? Now, that's something that we still discuss today but … um … was the debate which … uh … separated the thinking of Plato from his student, Aristotle.

Part 2: Track 65

Um, so what was life like as a medieval student? Well, some of the differences have already become apparent. You didn't have a set building that you studied in. You travelled to listen to the ideas and thinking of different masters. Students could travel all over Europe, many students did. Um, John of Salisbury, for example, managed to be a student for … many, many years … uh … travelling to different parts of Europe.

Students would go into university much younger than you guys, about 14, 15 years old. So what their— their foundational knowledge would be much lower than what we would expect here at university today.

Books were really expensive. There was no grand library for students to go and do research in. They were very dependent on what they were taught by their master. Students were very unlikely to own books and masters probably only owned a few books. So communication did depend on an oral interaction. All the teaching was in Latin and that meant that students could confidently travel all over Europe to hear the best lectures. It also meant, of course, that education was an elite activity. It required you not only to have money and to have the free time to be travelling, but also to have the language skills to allow you to do that.

Of course, it was also a very male-dominated environment. In fact, quite a misogynistic environment probably, of wine, women and song. And certainly, these young and potentially hot-headed scholars got themselves into trouble more than once. We have quite a lot of records of fights breaking out between students and people living in the town. They're called 'town and gown riots' and the most famous one is the St Scholastica Day Riot in Oxford in 1355, when 63 scholars and 30 locals died in a— a very large bout of fisty-cuffs. Another thing that was very expensive, was candles. So— … um … classes would start with the light. I don't know how much it appeals to you, to think that you might have to start class at 5 a.m. I'm certainly glad that I don't have to start lecturing at that time.

Now, I said I was going to come back to how we know that student life was like that. Because we have sources but they are not the level of records that we have today. Universities did not even have records in the same way because they were not organized, cohered institutions, certainly not in their very early years. So what sorts of things do we have? Well, we have a variety of different sources that we can use to piece things together.

One of the things that we have is early, legal documents about the university. So a particularly notable example of this is the statutes for Paris University, which were … um … issued by Papal Bull— … uh … Papal Commission in 1215. Um, and these are a set of rules which set out all sorts of things about university life. What you'll notice about them is that it's much more about the pragmatics of life than a modern university document, which probably has all sorts of … uh … good intentioned goals but they'll be really quite abstract. These statues— statutes reflect a very small community in which scholars and student— sorry, scholars and masters really knew each other well. So for example, in these statutes, if … uh … one of the students die, half of the masters in the university would go to their funeral. And if a master died, everybody would go. Of course, this seems a little strange to us but if you bear in mind the St Scholastica Day riots that I was mentioning earlier, you might realize that the risk of dying in the medieval period was somewhat higher than it is today.

The statutes also set out things like what texts would be studied. Which texts of Aristotle, for example, could and could not be studied. Very controversial. Um, they set out rules about who could be a master. They said that nobody was allowed to be a lecturer before they were twenty years old, and they must have studied for six years by then. Of course nowadays, becoming a y— a lecturer by twenty years old is not very realistic. However, if you were lecturing in … uh … Theology…

Chapter 9 Understanding your notes

Track 66
See dialogues in Chapter 9.

Track 67

PJ	Come in.
Inghar	Hello Professor Jackson. How are you?
PJ	Fine. Come in. Sit down. <Rustling as Inghar takes papers out of bags> Did you have a look at the notes I gave you on your essay structure?
Inghar	Yes, I did. Thank you. I've printed them off and I've got a few questions if that's okay.
PJ	Of course. Although I think the key thing is that your structure really lacks detail, so there's only so much I can comment on. Please try to resubmit another one with a lot more detail on your evidence and let me know what references you're going to use.
Inghar	Yes, I'm really sorry about that. I didn't realize it should be more detailed.
PJ	Well, the more detailed your plan is, the more advice I can give you. I think we'll also need to talk about your title.
Inghar	Yes, that was one of my questions. I have so much to write about! Do you think it's too broad?

PJ	Yes, quite possibly. It's an interesting title, but maybe you could narrow it by referring to only one animal instead of all mammals? I think you'll still have more than enough to write.
Inghar	Sorry did you say narrow it down to one animal?
PJ	Yes.
Inghar	Do you have any suggestions which one?
PJ	That's up to you, but more has been written about on primates than other kinds of mammal. So think about focusing on one of those.
Inghar	Yes, I will do. Primates. Thank you. Also I did include a list of books that I want to refer to. Do you think the list is full enough?
PJ	Have you read all of this list yet?
Inghar	Not yet, only the first three.
PJ	Well, I would revise the list if I were you to take into account your new title. This will be too broad now. Except for Hammerseid and Phillpotts. They'll give you some good pointers on where your further research should lie.
Inghar	Thanks so much.
PJ	I'll send you a couple of other sources which might come in handy too, but I'll need your new title before I can do that.
Inghar	Thanks so much.
PJ	Do you have any more questions?
Inghar	Just a couple. I wanted to ask you about my previous assignment …<fade>

Track 68

1 I think Steinman's theory is quite relevant for today's climate.

2 I'm in two minds about how relevant it is. I think we could apply it to the East, but not really to the West.

Track 69

Professor	So, we know that Durkheim, the godfather of Functionalist theory, says that education is a moralizing and socializing tool. What do you guys think about that?
Student 1	Well, I think to an extent it could be true, but it really depends on the education system.
Student 2	Yes, I agree. A lot of Western schools focus much more on the individual rather than the collective, which I think was the idea behind functionalism. To be a moralizing and socializing yardstick and help create an ordered society. Is that right?
Professor	Well, to an extent… We'll look at that later, but… go on…
Student 2	Well, lots of schools focus on the individual. Individual achievement and so on. This doesn't really point towards a collective… rather a more selfish belief.
Student 3	No, I think the socialization is more subliminal than that. Look at what school does in every country. You have to turn up on time, you have to obey the teacher. All of these

	things mirror what you have to do as an adult, obey rules, go to work on time, that sort of thing… pay your taxes!
Student 4	Yes, and social placement still goes on… which I think Parsons, Davis and Moore talked about
Professor	Yes
Student 4	Well, people are still ordered in school. Some go to university, some leave and get jobs.
Student 1	But is this really placement? I mean does a university education place you in a more beneficial role.
Prof	Actually, there are some good statistics on that which were referred to in the lecture….

Track 70
Kate

There are a few differences about what we call things in the States compared to the UK. Firstly, we don't use "tutorial" so much. We might 'get tutoring', which would mean working one on one with someone to improve our understanding of a topic. I guess that one-on-one meeting could be called a tutorial, but I don't feel that term is used so much in American colleges. We actually use it more with elearning and say, 'Take this online tutorial before you attend the in-person training'.

A seminar is pretty much the same, we usually mean a class with 10–20 people in it, focusing on reading texts and discussing them. We contrast a seminar with a lecture class, which would have up to a few hundred in it and just be a teacher talking, with very little discussion.

And when most Americans talk about University Life, they often say 'college life' as college is how we refer to an undergraduate degree. Young Americans ask each other 'Where did you go to college?' more than 'Where did you go to university?' Although the answer to the where did you go to college could be 'To Duke University'.

Track 71
Bob

Our terms are quite different to the UK and America, and the terms can change by subject too. Within something like engineering, a tutorial is usually just working through problems. This can be done in an individual tutorial or in groups. Kind of like what you might do in a maths class in high school. In a subject like law, a tutorial usually involves discussing various law points that have been set. In a history tutorial, you'd be talking about points that you are covering in your study. Tutorial classes can be any size really, typically they range from 10 to 30 students.

In my experience, the word seminar isn't really used. To me it's more like presenting, but we don't really use it. Lectures are the same as the UK. There's not much discussion in a lecture, if any, and the lecture groups are really large.

Track 72
Polly

I do biology at my university, we have lectures and tutorials, but also labs… which is basically a laboratory session where you can see an experiment or demonstration of something practical. I would say it's somewhere between a lecture and a tutorial really. The academic or teaching assistant at the front will introduce what we're going to do and sometimes demonstrate the first bit. They might ask some questions and then we do it ourselves. Demonstrators come around every so often to check we're doing it right. They might call the students round to show the next part sometimes. Again, they might ask some questions here. Sometimes the demonstrator will do everything, and the students just have to watch and listen. Sometimes afterwards you'll have a group tutorial with a demonstrator to discuss the lab session.

Track 73

Extract A

Professor Colby	So, I've had a look at your work and your main body is quite strong.
Student	Thank you, Professor. I worked pretty hard on it.
Professor C	The only thing I would say is that your referencing could do with some fine tuning.
Student	Yes, thank you. I'm not too sure about that area. What do you think I could do?
PC	Well, I'd just double check that you've referenced everything you need to. The course handbook should help you.
Student	Thank you

Extract B
[corridor noise]

Student	Excuse me, Dr Dexter. Could you answer a few questions about my essay please?
DD	I'm afraid now isn't the best time.
Student	I'll be quick.
DD	Have you made an appointment?
Student	No
DD	If I were you, I'd run up to the office and get one. I have two slots left this week and they'll go quick. I'm afraid I can't deal with them now. I really must go now.
Student	Okay, thanks.

Extract C

Student 1	I really enjoyed the lecture last week on the creative development of children. The reasons behind why it is so important were really interesting.
Student 2	Yes, I think that creative development is so essential in primary schools.
Professor	It is indeed, but perhaps it might be more useful to focus on the practical applications rather than the importance?
Student 3	Yes, I think the importance is really an established fact.
Student 1	I've got lots of ideas.
Professor	Excellent, well these are the types of things I think this session would be best used for.

Chapter 10 Moving forward

Track 74

Jing I find listening for long periods of time like in lectures really difficult. Even if I understand the topic well and have done the reading I just can't concentrate for an hour or more. It helps if the lecturer has an unusual speaking style or a loud voice. Otherwise I often feel like I'm getting lost in a mountain of information! Ha ha! There is one lecturer whose style I really like though 'cos she breaks up the lecture with interactive discussions with us. This helps me to concentrate and gives me a chance to process what she's saying better.

Albert When I'm in a lecture and I like the subject I don't have trouble listening, but when the topic is hard like about theories of learning or knowledge acquisition and the brain, it's difficult to listen and take notes at the same time. Sometimes I feel like I've missed an important point because I can't write quickly enough. But I suppose it's impossible to write down everything. I think I need to be more confident about that and focus on getting as much information as possible, then filling in the gaps through reading afterwards.

Susanna I really like lectures because I don't have to do any talking. My listening is much better than my speaking in English and I love finding out about all the different ideas about teaching, especially what academics thought in the past compared to now. The only problem I have is if the lecturer has a strong accent which I've never heard before. This can cause big problems for me because I'm used to hearing American English from TV and movies.

Track 75

Steffan So, I have to improve my listening for university in the UK. I've made a plan which you can see here and I'm going to do a lot in the next four months. The most important thing to do is practise so I'm going to listen to a lecture every day and take notes then ask my father to check for me 'cos he speaks English very well. From each lecture I want to make a list of all the new words and learn them to help develop my vocabulary. And for grammar I need to practise listening for typical grammar things like signposting language and tenses. I want to build this up over the months so at the end I can hear everything grammar related clearly. My teacher at school told me that I need to listen to different accents because I will probably have lecturers from different countries not just from the UK. This will be strange for me I think so I'm going to try accents like Indian, Chinese and Arabic. After that I think I'll be much more prepared for my university course, at least I hope so!

Track 76

Dr Roke Okay everyone, can you see the screen? Good. Right, well I want to look at study plans and how they match up with current thinking on how the brain functions when storing data. Then we can evaluate the effectiveness of study plans, which relates to your teaching practice. Here we have a study plan from Steffan. First, I want to draw your attention to the strength in the plan and this is repetition. By repeating the listening and vocabulary activities on a daily basis over four months he's likely to notice some improvement due to reinforcement theory. However, Steffan will find it difficult to notice the improvements if he does not use some kind of measurement tool such as testing himself. This will add significantly to the plan. The plan at the moment doesn't really fit with what we know about effective learning because there's no way of measuring what Steffan has learnt. Also, there's a problem with content. At the moment Steffan is only focusing on aspects of language at word and grammar level, rather than ideas and meaning. Even if he can recognize the grammar in the plan and increases his vocabulary will he be able to take effective notes on complex ideas and their relationships? Mmm, indeed, I suspect not and this may come as a shock when he starts his degree. So, what advice would we give Steffan? Well, remember last week when we talked about tracking progress through learner diaries? This would be a good idea to help Steffan monitor his progress. So, after each lecture he could write some notes in the diary about how much he understood, what aspects were difficult etc. and then read this before the next lecture to remind himself of what to focus on.

Track 77
See sentences in Chapter 10, Exercise 7.

Track 78

1 So, one of the key aspects of using action research is to be clear why this methodology is being implemented.

2 You know, although some still believe Drummond's theory on teaching practice, it's difficult to see how it works in modern teaching contexts.

3 Let's now turn to an example of, of politics ... sorry policy and how government policies affect the curriculum.

4 We've been mainly looking at child education so far this semester so next week we'll be expanding this into adult training.

5 What can we learn from this study? Well, firstly that detailed feedback is necessary for students to progress in their writing.

6 Today's lecture is gonna address some of the factors that you ought to be thinking about for your research project.

7 Now, this idea of classroom management can be used to address student behaviour in a variety of ways.

8 One of the things we are not going to cover is educational psychology because it's outside the scope of today's session.

9 Can you all see the graph on this slide? Okay, in that case let's analyse it some more.

10 There are several points here: student motivation, teacher motivation and the ethos of the institution.

Authentic lecture 5: Learner autonomy

Track 79

> To become better learners it's also important to reflect on the learning process itself and to draw attention to the processes involved. Much work has been done on learning styles and trying to identify your learning style or learning styles. Perhaps the most famous questionnaire and labelling system is Honey and Mumford's and ... um ... uh ... they use the labelling systems, activist, reflector, theorist and pragmatist amongst others. There are other labelling systems which ... um ... I have lif— listed here. Basically, the way it works is that you— you— you fill out a questionnaire and it is identified— ... uh ... what is identified is, how you like to learn, how you like to absorb information. And there are various versions but Honey and Mumford is probably the most famous.

More recently, Howard Gardner's Theory of Multiple Intelligences has become influential in this field. So in Howard Gardner's theory, everyone is intelligent in different ways, which will affect how they learn. And he's identified seven intelligences: musical, bodily-kinaesthetic, logical— mathematical, linguistic, spatial, interpersonal, intrapersonal. So you'll see these on the— these seven on the next slide. So ... um ... you know— I— I'm— I won't go through and read each of these out to you but in your own time please feel free to look into these more. Um, Howard Gardner has also— although he has identified these seven intelligences, he's also open to the possibility that there may be more.

So ... um ... on this slide you can see the seven intelligences that Howard Gardner has identified. So I'll quickly ... um ... run through some of these. The first one, interpersonal, in the top right corner, is about sensitivity the moo— to the moods and feelings of others and it enables us to work with others and listen effectively. So you might find that you— ... um ... this is one of the ... um ... intelligences that you feel that you have. The next one is musi— musical: the ability to perceive, appreciate and produce rhythm and pitch. It means you have a good ear and you are able to re— reproduce a tune. Spatial: a three dimensional, relational sense which enables us to perceive the worl— the visual world accur— accurately. It enables thinking in pictures, seeing things in relationship to others. Intrapersonal is self-knowledge and understanding of our own feelings, allows us to reflect on our own— on our experiences and learn from them. Linguistic, you have sensitivity to sounds, rhythms and meanings of words and to language. Logical-mathematical, you have the ability to recognize numerical or logical patterns and to sort and analyse. And finally, bodily-kinaesthetic. This is— this is talking about the control of body movements and the capacity to handle objects skilfully. It ena— enables us to express ourselves physically and play games.

Um, while I've just gone through these seven, Howard Gardner has also said that ... um ... he is also open to the possibility that there may be more. There may be for example, the naturalist intelligent— intelligence— the naturalist intelligence. So for example, this would be the capacity to organize and categorize natural— the natural world. For example, plants, spe— plants or ... um ... insects into different species. So that's another possibility.

Throughout your courses, please try and reflect on the purpose of every activity you do. Think about the activity before you are about to do it, during you're doing the activity and afterwards. If you think about the purpose, this will help make the benefits of every activity that you do more apparent.

In conclusion, learner autonomy is grounded in cooperation and collaboration. It's formed through some of the techniques we've talked about today, such as needs analysis and discovering your learning styles. Incorporating some or a— or— or all of these techniques in your learning will increase your self-awareness so that you become better, more effective learners.

Answer key

Chapter 1

Exercise 1
1 D   2 B   3 C   4 A

Exercise 2
A
2 board   3 screens   4 overhead projectors
5 interactive white boards

B
6 lecture theatre   7 lectern   8 handouts   9 notes
10 discussion   11 presentations   12 tutorials

Exercise 3
1 discussion   2 board   3 handout   4 tutorial
5 interactive white board   6 lectern   7 screen
8 overhead projector   9 lecture theatre
10 note   11 a presentation

Exercise 4
Before the lecture

D   F   C

During the lecture

B   H   I

After the lecture

G   E   A

Exercise 5
1 Last week I went to a really interesting lecture on space but I didn't understand that much of it because I hadn't prepared enough.

2 One of the most important aspects of university study which is totally different from school is being able to manage the workload.

3 What I don't like about studying biology is having to write up the lab reports after doing the experiments.

4 So, if you look at this slide, you'll notice how the concepts of philosophy as described by the Enlightenment interact with our everyday lives, even in the 21st century.

Exercise 6
1 B   2 C   3 D   4 A

Exercise 7
1 both   2 both   3 informal   4 informal
5 formal   6 formal   7 both

Exercise 8
1 first/all   2 can /seen   3 end   4 key   5 real winner   6 two-way   7 implicit/party   8 well
9 look   10 build

Exercise 9
1 signposting   2 passive/hedging   3 phrasal verb   4 noun phrase   5 idiomatic   6 idiomatic
7 noun phrase   8 signposting   9 signposting
10 phrasal verb

Exercise 10
A is more formal. Use of: full verbs / passive / hedging.

B is more informal. Use of: phrasal verbs 'work out' / idiomatic language 'knock on effect'.

Exercise 11
Understanding your course

2, 3, 5

Helping with your assignments and assessments

1, 3, 4, 6

Chapter 2

Self evaluation
1 Not useful, although if you are interested in the topic it will not do any harm. Be prepared to change your views though as your lecturer may disagree with the ideas you've read about.

2 Useful, Other students may have other experiences of the topic that can help you focus on what might be important.

3 Not useful, at university you need to take an active role in your own learning so you cannot depend on the lecturer providing you with all the answers.

4 Both are possible, it depends what you read – always be careful when reading on the internet. Make sure what you read is from an academic source.

5 Useful, this will start to give you an idea of the topic and if it's from an academic text book it is likely to be a good starting point.

6 Useful, helps you to focus on the lecture.

Exercise 1

Students' own answers.

Exercise 2

1 Modules 1 and 4 because of the word introduction

2 Modules 2 and 5 because they are more theoretical so are likely to be more academic and contain complex ideas

Exercise 3

Module 1 Thomas, Module 2 Thomas, Module 3 Walters, Module 4 Fredrickson, Module 5 Fredrickson, Module 6 Brown

Exercise 4

1 Students' own answers **2** Students' own answers **3** they help you to process the information and remember it

Exercise 5

Suggested answers:

1 look up definitions and examples of each type of media **2** check EU member countries **3** check EU election results post 2000 **4** read examples of each media **5** watch/read media coverage of an election **6** discuss ideas with other students **7** look at the reading list, identify useful readings and read them

Exercise 6

Good ideas: Focus your reading on the specific lecture topic. Restrict your reading to one or two chapters of a book. Check the meaning of new words or phrases in a dictionary.

Exercise 7

1 C **2** B **3** D **4** A **5** E

Exercise 8

2 Core module **3** Journal **4** Optional module **5** Course outline **6** Reading list **7** Elective **8** Core textbook

Exercise 9

See audio script on page 150 for answers.

Exercise 10

Speaker 2

Exercise 11

So what we have here is an example of a policing policy// which could be responsible for an area's crime statistics,// however it is difficult to say for sure// because this is a new approach// which may require time to provide a clear picture.

It's important to remember that demographics are dynamic,// by that I mean that people and places are constantly in a state of change,//so don't rely on data that is more than 5 years old// if you are focusing on urban areas or towns// which have received a recent influx of inhabitants.

Exercise 12

1 B **2** E **3** A **4** C **5** F **6** D **7** H **8** G **9** F **10** E **11** G **12** B **13** A **14** H **15** C **16** D

Exercise 13

Lecture 1: Giving examples, (to name a few), Showing importance, (I'd like to draw your attention to),

Lecture 2: Summarizing, (overall), Clarifying or summarizing, (as I've just said), Giving examples (things like),

Lecture 3: Finishing a point, (we're going to leave … for now), Showing contrast, (opposing this view is)

Lecture 1: Bill Gates and philanthrocapitalism

Preparation 1

1 No **2** Yes **3** Yes **4** Yes **5** No **6** Yes

Preparation 2
The following words would be useful:

philanthropy, capitalism,
philanthrocapitalism

These are all words related to the title so you are likely to hear these in the lecture.

business

You probably know this word already, and after doing a bit of preparatory reading as suggested in Preparation 1, you have probably realized that it's likely that you will hear this word while listening to the lecture.

entrepreneur, billionaire

These words relate to Bill Gates so you might assume that you'll hear these in the lecture.

pledge, bilingual, distinction

It's difficult to know if you'll hear these words in the lecture. They are not directly related to business or philanthropy.

Preparation 3
1 def: – h definition
2 uni – b university
3 w. – d with
4 cos – a because
5 q – g question
6 b – e born
7 CEO – c Chief Executive Officer
8 ed. – f education

Preparation 4
1 PhilCap – e Philanthrocapitalism
2 BG – f Bill Gates
3 MSoft – c Microsoft
4 WB – b Warren Buffett
5 Comps – a computers
6 B + M – d Bill and Melinda

Authentic Lecture: Sample answers

Bill Gates	Microsoft founder/multi-billionaire/ entrepreneur + PHILANTHROPIST Involved in PhilCap
Background	b. 1955 Seattle Affluent family mother was a philanthropist too poss influence? →
Education	13 yrs old – Lakeside Prep Sch started liking comps → BG excelled at programming – gifted student Got into Harvard Uni BUT dropped out. BG said that timing/ideas meant he had to start getting into industry. (Doesn't recommend dropping out to others)
Microsoft	1975 started, w. Paul Allen 2000 left as CEO 2008 left completely
~~PhilCap~~ Bill + Melinda Gates Foundation	Focus on aids, malaria, poverty and ed ed in USA Mission: mix tech advances w. people who need it most Slogan: All lives have equal value 2010: talked about foundation w. journalist – why chose these issues? Cos health has stabilising effect. In USA greatest inequality in edu. Def: act of giving/doing sth for poor people/giving to good causes

Philanthropy	Def: business person who believes business has a duty to give back / believe business better poised to deliver philanthropy
PhilCap	BG: Vaccines one of best investments in giving. (best return + best chance of saving lives) this is for example: of business + philanthropy
Giving Pledge	Formed by BG and Warren Buffett 2010
	What is it? Get billionaires to give ½ of wealth to good causes No contact but public verbal commitment People who agreed incl Mark Zuckerberg (Fbook) Info on website Got 100 USA billionaires, now focusing on billionaires around the world
B+M Foundation	WB has pledged. Want to inspire people to give back. Everyone should do this. Q for me: Would I do this when successful?

Reflection

Are full sentences used? Why/why not? No, it saves time when writing to leave out words like articles. Remember not to leave out words which might affect the meaning.

Why is the last sentence underlined? The last sentence is underlined because the student has to do something after the lecture. This might help the student remember.

Are there mistakes in the notes? What kind? There are mistakes (crossing out). It is impossible to not make any mistakes. You might think the lecturer is going to talk about something, and then they don't. Just cross it out and move on. Sometimes you will make spelling mistakes. Don't worry about this.

What can you do if you can't spell a word? Don't worry. Just spell it as best you can and make sure you look the word up or ask someone how it is spelled after the lecture. This is likely to happen with names when you can't see them on the screen.

Chapter 3

Self Evaluation
1 F 2 T 3 F 4 T 5 T

Exercise 1
Possible answers:

1 Future of global warming/predictions   2 Definition of alternative energy   3 Wind/water

What other ways could this information be presented?

Possible answers:

Lecture 1 now, past, future
Lecture 2 definition, why needed, examples in any order

Exercise 2
1 C 2 E 3 A 4 F 5 H 6 B 7 G 8 D

Exercise 3
1 D 2 B 3 G 4 E 5 F 6 H 7 C 8 A

Exercise 4
Has been talked about

2, 3, 7, 9

Will be talked about next

4, 6

Will be talked about later

1, 5, 10

Exercise 5
1 description/explanation
2 situation/problem/solution/evaluation

Exercise 6
e, a, c, b, d, f

Exercise 7
e, b, c, a, d, f

Exercise 8
1 Anterior surface 2 Constricted pupil
3 Pupillary ruff 4 Contraction furrows
5 Collarette 6 Crypts of Fuchs

Exercise 9
1 Summarizing, Recommending further study

2 Recommending further study, Offering questions

3 Offering questions, Giving assignments

From lectures

1 Alternative energy lecture 2 Planetary
Discovery 3 Deep Sea Exploration: Effects on
delicate ecosystems

Exercise 10
1 is, have, all. 2 is/have, change to past or
negative, all change in quantity 3 Students' own
answers.

Exercise 11
1 's been/will have/most 2 is/haven't
3 was/have/none 4 was/had/one

Chapter 4

Self-evaluation
Students' own answers.

Exercise 1
1 American 2 No 3 No, South
African 4 Strong

Exercise 2
1 b 2 d 3 a 4 c

Exercise 3
Students' own answers

Exercise 4
Students' own answers

Exercise 5
Students' own answers

Exercise 6
1 Today's lecture is going to touch on some of the
key theories of game theory.

2 So, you can see that this experiment hasn't
provided much useful data.

3 Astronomers have tried to discover what the
exact function of Saturn's rings are.

4 The soil in this region is so porous that it is
unlikely that any plants will be able to get their
roots to take hold.

Exercise 7
Content

use of slides, visual information, use of diagrams,
handouts

Delivery

asks students questions, reading a prepared script,
includes discussion, conversational

Exercise 8
Lecturer 1 reading a prepared script

Lecturer 2 includes discussion

Lecturer 3 conversational

Exercise 9
1 ✗ 2 ✓ 3 ✗ 4 ✗ 5 ✓ 6 ✓ 7 ✓ 8 ✓

A 3 B 4 C 1

Exercise 10
Students' own answers

Lecture 2: A brief overview of tsunamis

Preparation 2
a No. People's ideas on tsunamis are unlikely to be
important for this overview.

b Yes

c Unlikely. It's an overview, so there won't be too much detail.

d Yes

e Yes

f Yes

g Unlikely. The lecture is focusing on tsunamis, not natural disasters in general. (Only if they are connected)

Preparation 3
Likely order:

b, e, d, f

Authentic Lecture: Part 1
A definition of tsunamis

1 Generation 2 Propagation 3 Land fall

Authentic Lecture: Part 2 sample answers
Slide 15

2.2. Deep water theory doesn't apply to the **deep ocean.** tsun in deep ocean follow shallow water theory bec. **depth** much less than **wavelength.**

Slide 16

2.3 Speed of the waves = **700** kilometres per hour = speed of a **jet plane.**

* REMEMBER THIS EQUATION FOR THE EXAM.

Reflection

Why does the student write only summaries of the slides? Because a lot of the information is already on the slides, so the student really needs to get the general ideas and make sure he/she has a copy of the slides.

Why has the student written numbers before his summary? So he/she can match them to the numbers on the slides. This means he can keep track of his notes.

What does tsun and bec. mean in the students notes? Tsunami and because.

Did the student try to write everything down? No, it would be too difficult and a lot of the information is on the slides.

Chapter 5

Self Evaluation
1 F 2 T 3 T 4 F 5 T 6 F

Exercise 1
Key fact

Landmark dates in mobility (immigration) law, Economic effects of immigration upon the host country, Definition of worker mobility, References to books on worker mobility, Effects of emigration upon the country of origin, Factors effecting mobility decisions

Not key fact

Story about worker mobility in a newspaper, Lecturer's experience of moving countries for his job, Definition of work

Could be in both areas

A list of the most popular countries to move to

Exercise 2
Students' own answers

Suggested answers:
indicators show economic decline, real indicator is the yield curve

Exercise 3
One type of worker satisfaction is based on employer drivers – these are the things that employers provide for their employees. We call this extrinsic motivation because it is kind of outside the control of the employee, <u>they have to take whatever the company offers.</u> So, there are four main drivers here. Salary and benefits are the most important as no one wants to work for free! <u>People apply for jobs based on the money they're going to earn.</u> A close second is the type of work as people want to be stimulated by what they're going to do for 40 hours or more a week. <u>Studies by Smith and Thompson have noted that one of the key reasons for leaving a job is monotony and the lack of fulfilment.</u> The next two are also related – it's human nature to want to progress in life so promotion and training are key factors in making sure workers are happy. <u>This is perhaps why continual professional development has played such a key role in many companies for the last twenty years.</u>

(shaded) = main point

___ = supporting point

Exercise 4
Students' own answers

Exercise 5

TYPE OF COMPANY STRUCTURE

– Sole trader / partnership

– Limited company (Public or private)

– Co-operative

TARGETING VIRAL MARKETING

3 principles:

– Gathering social profiles

– Proximity marketing

– Key word analysis

Exercise 6
Fact

In the UK the tax rate for corporations is 20% of profits. There are a number of ways in which corporations can reduce their tax bill but all companies pay corporation tax unless they make a loss in any given tax year

although Sachs's theory can apply here

Opinion

According to Taylor we need to think more carefully about how the rules work in practice taxation

Certain economists believe that Sachs has overlooked some fundamental calculations. The interpretations from other economists suggest that small businesses should expect slower growth in all economic climates but to my mind this is an incomplete picture and needs further clarification

Suggested answers:
Use of present simple and theory for factual information.

Use of according to, interpretations, believe, to my mind for opinions.

Exercise 7
1 F   2 O   3 F

Exercise 8
1 C   2 A   3 B

Exercise 9
1 D   2 A   3 E   4 C   5 B

Exercise 10
1 long term, not short term/ especially, emphasizing how hard/ no way, not even a small chance/ new… small, these types of company not other types/enough, they will have some but maybe not enough

2 not entirely, slightly clear but not completely/ how, we don't know in what way/ are, in contrast to not entirely clear/ in theory, maybe not in reality/some, we don't know how much

3 so, emphasis to show how large/ forced, they have no choice/ really, or just slightly effective

Exercise 11
1 could, not

2 must, have

Exercise 12
1 B

2 A

Exercise 13
2 risk analysis

3 to be properly prepared

4 possible problems

5 developing a strategic plan to tackle them

6 the company

7 academics in general

Exercise 14

1 the students and the lecturer of the course

2 people in general

3 academics in general, the students in the lecture, the academics in the department of the university.

Chapter 6

Self-evaluation

1 F 2 T 3 F 4 T 5 F 6 F 7 T

Exercise 1

Mohammed

Retail in the UK, Challenges for retail

Samuel

An overview of key marketing strategies

Yuen

Online stores

Exercise 2

1 b 2 j 3 f 4 a 5 i 6 c 7 g 8 d
9 h 10 e

Exercise 3

2 Response 3 Assumption 4 Situation
5 Biases 6 Evidence 7 Reasoning 8 Relevance

Exercise 4

1 wide reaching effects /these need to be taken quite carefully into consideration.

2 met with scepticism by his peers/giving scathing critiques.

3 ignores other possible factors, which really need to be addressed.

4 was writing this at a time when

5 comes from his socialist ideology

6 based this argument on the research /large sample /covered most demographic groups. / largest and most representative survey

7 fails to explain how he reaches this conclusion.

8 is particularly relevant to /theory applies specifically to this area.

Exercise 5

2 criticism 3 criticism 4 criticism 5 criticism
6 support 7 criticism 8 support

Exercise 6

Option 3: He shows bias towards the pharmaceutical company and has made assumptions that more supermarkets make more money. All arguments are based on poor reasoning.

Because one supermarket makes money, doesn't mean more will. Usually a town will have a finite amount of money for groceries and increasing their shopping choices doesn't necessarily mean they will buy more.

Dr Burns works in the pharmaceutical company so he may be biased in regards to their expansion.

The pharmaceutical company has a constant demand. This is different from a growing demand. There might not be any more demand if they expand.

Jobs might not necessarily go to people within the town.

Exercise 7

2 K positive 3 F positive 4 A positive
5 E negative 6 I negative 7 B positive
8 H negative 9 C positive 10 D negative
11 J negative

Exercise 8
Suggested answers:

seminal = Smith's work wasn't very original…,We couldn't call Smith's work seminal…

ground-breaking = Smith's work wasn't very original…/ looked over old ground/ really a reinforcement of/ adhered to the thought of the da

questionable = Smith's work is unquestionable…/ What makes Smith's work doubtless is…/ Smith's work is undisputed…/ Smith's work can't be called into question…

incomplete = Smith's theory is complete…/ This is a comprehensive theory…

objective = Smith's is very subjective in…/ Smith may be lacking objectivity…./ Smith's objectivity is called into question…

inaccurate = Smith's data may be accurate…/ isn't inaccurate…/ is correct….

significant contributions = Smith makes insignificant contributions to…/ Smith's contributions aren't significant…/ Smith's minor contributions…./ These aren't substantial contributions…

unconvincing = Smith's ideas are convincing…/ Smith's ideas are not unconvincing…/ Smith's ideas are persuasive…

misguided = Smith is sensible in..../ Smith isn't misguided in..../ Smith is reasonable in...

Exercise 9
1 negative   2 positive

Exercise 10
go/w/ and, lie/j/at

Exercise 11
1 /w/ /w/   2 /r/ /j/   3 /w/ /j/   4 /r/
5 /j/ /w/   6 /j/ /w/

Exercise 12
1 Education is key t**o** develo**p**ing th**e** workforce o**f** th**e** futu**re a**nd this is recognized in th**e** theories o**f** Jens**o**n which we'll be discussing lat**er** on.

2 What we c**a**n see fr**o**m this analysis is th**a**t teach**er** training varies throughout th**e** world except in internati**o**nal schools which maintain **a** fixed curricul**u**m.

3 Becoming an independ**e**nt learn**er** should be th**e** goal **o**f any university stud**e**nt as this will raise your confid**e**nce **a**nd allow you t**o** make progress fast**er**.

Exercise 13
1 C   2 A   3 B   4 A

Lecture 3: The pursuit of innovation

Preparation 1
- Read the definition, overview and key ideas on the handout to familiarize yourself with the subject.
- Look up the meaning of unknown words
- Follow up on the further reading list on the handout. Read the pages mentioned.
- Try and predict the kind of information that the lecturer is going to cover.

Preparation 2
1 No. This is not relevant to the lecture.

2 Yes. The lecturer is likely to include information about the past situation.

3 Maybe.

4 Yes. This is some of the main content of the lecture.

5 Maybe. This may be included as background information.

6 Maybe. The lecturer may talk about people but may only talk about companies.

7 Maybe. The lecturer may talk about legal aspects but this may not be relevant.

8 No. The lecturer will assume that the audience knows the meaning of this.

9 No. This is not relevant.

10 Maybe. The lecturer may talk about the future or this may be the subject of another lecture.

Preparation 3
innovation / innovate
An innovation is a new thing or a new method of doing something.

To innovate means to introduce changes and new ideas in the way something is done or made.

R and D
The part of a commercial company's activity concerned with applying the results of scientific research to develop new products and improve existing ones.

interactive
An interactive computer program or television system is one which allows direct communication between the user and the machine.

networked
When a television or radio programme is networked, it is broadcast at the same time by several different television companies.

implications
The implications of something are the things that are likely to happen as a result.

model (n)
A model of an object is a physical representation that shows what it looks like or how it works.

draw on
If you draw on or draw upon something such as your skill or experience, you make use of it in order to do something.

non-disclosure agreement
A legally enforceable contractual agreement in which somebody agrees not to reveal or disclose information to a third party.

be aligned with something
If you align yourself with a particular group, you support them because you have the same political aim.

brands
A brand of a product is the version of it that is made by one particular manufacturer.

facilities
Facilities are buildings, pieces of equipment, or services that are provided for a particular purpose.

implement an idea
If you implement something such as a plan, you ensure that what has been planned has been done.

Authentic lecture sample answers

What mean 4 indiv.? NOT organ.

V diff if YOUR job = go 2 get new ideas

Probs = **1** colleagues NOT like ext ideas

    2 Ideas NOT aligned to company processes

    3 NOT not line up with your skills

    4 Take a while to exploit.

    5 Costs a lot

Result = many org. turn away from **ext ideas**

BUT now = people hunting 4 the merits

    Find rel. w/ people 2 **explore new ideas**

Chall. 4 trad R&D orgs

Manage new model = openness

Need people who know

    1 how 2 build rel.

    2 how 2 talk re: IP

    3 when 2 talk about **ND agr*.**

    Indiv have to acquire these skills

Our research: **diff indiv. roles in innov process.**

Research topic = large org & roles of different R&D staff in bringing in knowledge

Findings = 3 roles that indiv. take up

    1 Explorers – actively searching 4 new ideas

    2 Some indiv good @assim ideas into company – enthuse other people

    3 Some = good @ selling ext. ideas internally

Some take on all 3 & some – none

Result of our res: indiv who take on all 3 = **highest individual performance**

Conclusions: Not enough to just explore the ext. space.

Need to think about how ideas will B assim & **driven through company until produced.**

* ND agr. = non-disclosure agreement

Chapter 7

Self-evaluation

1 Bad 2 Good 3 Bad 4 Good 5 Bad 6 Bad

Exercise 1

List

Advantages = simple, students choose how much to write. Disadvantages = doesn't show how ideas relate to each other.

Cornell

Advantages = free, makes students review their work. Disadvantages = only works with organized students who follow the system.

Outline

Advantages = shows how ideas relate to each other (uses colours and arrows), easier for students to read and understand notes after lectures. Disadvantages = only works for students with good listening skills who can organize points well. Difficult if lecturer speaks fast or delivers content in a random way.

Mapping

Advantages = shows how ideas relate to each other (uses colours and arrows), easier for students to read and understand notes after lectures. Disadvantages = doesn't work for everyone, bad for logical thinkers.

Exercise 2

1 Charting because there are four separate areas which the lecturer will probably talk about separately and they may not relate to each other.

2 List OR Outline because the info will be presented chronologically.

3 Mapping because there are a variety of factors which could be inter-related.

4 Mapping OR Cornell because the info is likely to be inter-related.

Exercise 3
Example outline

> Mark Twain Feb 21st
>
> 1 Early life:
>
> Family – 6 children, youngest, troublemaker, Dad died when 12 yrs
>
> Schooling – left at 12
>
> Work – printer, journalist, river pilot, army, writer
>
> 2 Literary work:
>
> Influences – hometown, southern life, trads, frontier life, slavery, financial probs., classical writers e.g. Pliny, nature
>
> Major works – Huck Finn & Tom Sawyer

Exercise 4
1 d 2 g 3 j 4 h 5 i 6 c 7 o 8 n 9 e
10 m 11 a 12 p 13 k 14 l 15 f 16 b

Exercise 5
1 c 2 d 3 e 4 b 5 a

Exercise 6

Abbreviation	Word	Abbreviation	Word
Info	Information	sthg	Something
poss	Possibility/ possibly	re:	Regarding/ about/ concerning
diff	Different/ difficult	max	Maximum
int	Interesting	Q	Question
Probs	Problems	approx.	Approximately
imp	Important	min	Minimum
s/o	Someone	incl	Including
prob	Probability/ probably	v.	Very
esp	Especially	bec	Because
A	Answer	w/	With
w/o	Without	ref	Reference

Exercise 7
Suggested answers:

> Poss probs w/ birth certs c.19 Engl.
>
> 1 Many forged docs bec. of names only on census @ time.
>
> 2 Diff 2 follow fam trees ∴ spelling. % of lit pop = low ∵ officials guessed spelling, esp foreign e.g. Fr & Dutch. → inaccuracies BUT int ↑ number of surnames. E.g Smith, Smithe etc.

Exercise 8
1 **Lina** focus on ideas she understands & wr clearly, names, dates, numbers & key terms or vocab from slides bec lecturer's e.g.s → read after. List then wr key words/ phrases + Gm trans.

2 **Gregor**

mapping and lists, colours, arrows 2 connect similar ideas. Don't wr 2 much bec imp 2 list & understand, always wr e.g.s bec useful.

3 **Ozan**
wr as much as poss, free style, rewr notes after, focus on quantity, reduce notes 2 main points w/ e.g.s & connections after.

Exercise 9
Possible Answers

Extract 1 Main areas = reason, self, society

Origin = econ, trade, empire, ind rev, dipl, legal.

Main writers/ thinkers = Voltaire, Rousseau, smith and Kant.

Extract 2 Non standard e.g. hols, training, childcare←**Empl law** → standard e.g. sick pay/ mat leave See Cooke v Leyton

Extract 3 Pritchard = socioling & psycholing connected thru lang. ∴ gr & words study 1st.

C.f. both systems across lang families b/4 look @ key Qs.

Socio = infl. Lang on cult & vice versa

Psycho = where lang produced & how lang. Acquired

Exercise 10
Necessary 4, 5

Extra 1, 2, 3

Exercise 11

1 which/ extra
2 that or which/ necessary
3 who/ necessary
4 which/ extra

Exercise 12

1 Statements with multiple clauses
2 List
3 Asking and answering a question

Exercise 13

1 Rise-fall arrows on *Renaissance*/ fall arrow on *society in general*
2 Rise-fall arrows on *past 20 years*/ fall arrow on *modern society*
   Rise-fall arrows on *the lecture*/ fall arrow on *Surrealist art movement*

Chapter 8

Self-evaluation

1 ✓ Simon's comment is good because he is reviewing his notes directly after the lecture and it will give him time to think about the lecture and plan any follow up research.

2 ✗ Dorota's comment is not so good because when she rereads her notes later she may not remember the key points and she may not have done any follow up research.

3 ✗ Ali's comment is not so good because he does not have any follow up actions.

4 ✓ Sumita's comment is good because by discussing her notes with her friends she will be able to find any gaps in her notes and clarify points she didn't understand.

Exercise 1

Add the two names of the Nobel prize winners

Say why language, geography and religion were important

What does trans mean? It could be translate, transfer, transnational etc and complete the part after BUT

Give examples of the new structures

Specify what European ideas were rejected and what 'explore margins' means

Check reading list for full title, which chapters from which 6 books?

Exercise 2
Suggested answers:

3 He needs to fill in some details so he can match the relevant sections of his notes to his assessment.

4 He might waste time searching for the books and chapters.

5 If he doesn't know which chapters, he could spend too much time reading for his assessment.

Exercise 3

Make sure all folders are labelled in the same way – probably by semester, then module number & title so put all 3 module folders inside the semester folder and label each one with the module title too. Maybe separate by lecturer.

Rename all the documents to include the date and lecture title.

Maybe add the name of the lecturer too.

Make sure the reading list is in the folder with the module it corresponds to.

Exercise 4

1 module name/ date

2 highlight

3 further reading

4 chronological

5 module or topic

6 assessment

Exercise 5

> Ancient Rome
>
> Plato BC 4th & Aristotle BC ~~5th~~ 3rd
>
> citizens should focus on role in soc. – think about ~~money~~ abilities
>
> majority is imp & democ = ~~most~~ least dang form of gov.

<u>UK</u>

Document = Magna Carta 1215 – said ~~people~~ government must obey law.

Hobbes c16th: Democ won't work, govt should have power.

Locke c. ~~18th~~ 17th: contract bet people & govt. Govt protects people & have right 2 change govt

Wollstonecraft c.18th: all people equal, didn't bel in marriage

<u>France</u>

Montesquieu c. 17th: limit monarchy, sep powers – basis of US constitution, relig v ~~good~~ bad 4 soc.

Voltaire c. 17th: bel in reason → progress, govt good if people prot by laws, democ ok 4 ~~large~~ small countries.

Rousseau c. 18th:

Rule belongs 2 people ~~BUT people can do nthg they can rise up & change govt~~ – ideas 4 Fr Rev

Suggested answers:

- 3rd: 4th century mentioned first so Roberto could have thought 5th would be next.

- Money: both abilities and money are mentioned so Roberto could have confused the positive and the negative.

- Government: it's more usual for people to obey/ break the law. This mistake could have come from a short lack of concentration.

- 17th: Roberto could have made this mistake from writing quickly – the names and dates are close together in the recording.

- rel v bad 4 soc: this mistake prob happened because Roberto heard the word 'good' but not the negative 'didn't think' that came before it.

- Small: It is likely that Roberto didn't hear the negative in 'aren't large'.

- They can rise up & change govt: the lecturer says 'does nothing' so Roberto could have connected this to people instead of the government.

Exercise 6
Suggested answer:
Step 1:

Lecture 2: Latin American lit c20.

Nobel prize winners = 5 (Mistral, Marquez, Vargas...)

Themes in fiction

   political hist = big infl on writers

      indigenous heritage = v. imp bec of sthg about individual countries

Lang, geog and religion also imp.

New style of wr comp to Europe

   Original bec. no established rules

      Trans BUT also …

New structures

   Writing about rural & urban life v. diff

For example: 1 **Borges & Argentina – Reject Euro ideas**

      Focus on good writing

      Explore margins

Reading = Borges: a writer …. (sthg about culture – check reading list) + some chapters from 6 books

Step 2:

1 Read about similarities too because the essay says totally distinct and some themes may be present in European lit too.

2 Read about themes in detail

3 Need to find 2 or 3 other writers – Borges not enough.

4 Need specific book(s) from Borges and other writers.

Step 3:

1 1 or 2 days for research + 2 or 3 days for reading.

2 1–2 days per theme

3 1 or hours to choose relevant writers.

4 Half a day to select specific books.

Exercise 7

> **Key Philosophers & Democracy**
>
> 1 Anc Rome: Plato BC 4th & Aristotle BC 5th
>
>   Pl = citizens should focus on role in soc. – det. by wealth
>
>   Ar =maj is supreme & democ least dang form of gov.
>
> 2 UK: Magna Carta 1215 – said people must obey law.
>
>   Hobbes c16th: Democ won't work, govt should have power.
>
>   Locke c. 18th: contract bet people & govt. Govt protects & people have right 2 change it
>
>   Wollstonecraft c.18th: all people equal, didn't bel in marriage
>
> 3 France
>
>   Montesquieu c. 17th: limit monarchy, sep powers – basis of US constitution, rel. v imp. 4 soc
>
>   Voltaire c. 17th: bel in reason → progress, govt good if people prot by laws, democ ok 4 large countries.
>
>   Rousseau c. 18th: corruption changes indiv bec not enough power
>
>   Rule belongs 2 people BUT people can do noth – ideas 4 Fr Rev
>
>   Social Contract 1762 'Man is born free, yet everywhere he is in chains'.

Step 2:

1 Need more detail on each of the 4 philosophers – summary of key ideas (1 slide per philosopher). Ideally 2 or 3 books which compare & contrast.

2 Choose 1 to research in detail – prob Rousseau?

3 Read about how his ideas match modern politics. Need specific books here.

Step 3:

1 1 day to get overview of their ideas

2 1 day to write summaries

3 2–3 days to research Rousseau

4 2–3 days to relate ideas to modern politics and prep analysis.

Exercise 8

1 The age of Romanticism

2 the purpose of art galleries

3 the role of poverty

4 an analysis of the text

5 the thinking of Plato

Exercise 9

Fright

The word **fear** because it is connected to fright NOT flight. Even though you might think you heard flight because of the bird the context of the lecture is about fossils which helps you understand the last word correctly.

Exercise 10

1 match (the speaker says mash)

2 The speaker is talking about connections, cause and effect, being logical, finding items that are the same so the word is likely to be match as this is a synonym.

Lecture 4: The history of universities in Western Europe

Preparation 1

1 scholar = A scholar is a person who studies an academic subject and knows a lot about it.

2 dialogue = A communication or discussion between people or groups of people such as governments or political parties.

3 master (n) = If you say that someone is a master of a particular activity, you mean that they are extremely skilled at it.

4 debate = A debate is a discussion about a subject on which people have different views.

5 Latin = Latin is the language which the ancient Romans used to speak.

6–10 Students' own answers.

Preparation 2
Sample answers:

dialogue – d/log

master – mstr

debate – this one might not be useful to shorten as the letters can commonly form lots of words (for example: dbt could also be doubt)

Latin – Lat

Authentic lecture: Part 2 sample answers

What was life like as a medieval student?

Authentic lecture: Part 1 sample answers

> Classical learning – sophisticated. Avail only to men.
>
> VESPASIAN (Emporor) understood importance of a 1. **well educated** popn
>
> Learning done through DIALECTICS – still done now (definition: 2.**establishing** sth is **correct/true via dialogue with** ppl **who have** diff **views**)
>
> e.g the nature of **universals**: "is goodness in single acts or in the abstract?" discussed in Plato's time and today.
>
> **Follow up**
>
> | | |
> |---|---|
> | available | avail |
> | population | popn |
> | something | sth |
> | different | diff |
> | people | ppl |
> | for example | e.g. |

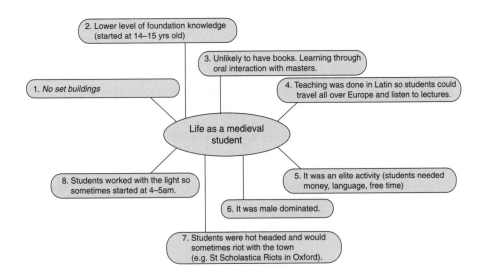

187

How do we know what life was like?

Early legal documents tell us a lot about university life. For example: Statutes for Paris University, 1215 Rules were quite pragmatic – for example: if a student dies, half the masters must go to their funeral / sets out the texts which must be studied / sets out the rules to being a master (masters must be over 20 years old etc.)

Chapter 9

Self-evaluation
1 T 2 F 3 T 4 F 5 T 6 F

Exercise 1
1 N 2 Y 3 Y 4 Y 5 N 6 N 7 Y
8 Y 9 Y 10 N

1 Your English language is not the responsibility of your subject tutor. They are responsible for your subject content.

5 Tutors may be able to give indications of how good your work is but grading is a formal process which must be done at the correct time.

6 You are responsible for your time management at university.

10 Your written work must be your own. You must not ask anyone to do it for you.

Exercise 2
1 Resubmit a more detailed structure/ plan (with evidence / references)

2 Narrow down the title (focus on one animal possibly primates)

3 Revise reading list to reflect title

Exercise 3
Asking for clarification – a, l

Asking for Repetition – h, k

Agreeing – g

Disagreeing – f, m

Expressing hesitation – d, f, o

Adding further information – b, i, j

Moving on – j, n

Giving an opinion – c, e

Exercise 4

Professor	So, we know that (Theorist:) <u>Durkheim</u>, the godfather of Functionalist theory, says that (Concept:) <u>education is a moralising and socialising tool.</u> What do you guys think about that?
Student 1	Well, I think to an extent it could be true, but it really depends on the education system.
Student 2	Yes, I agree. A lot of (against) <u>Western schools</u> focus much more on the individual rather than the collective, which I think was the idea behind functionalism. To be a moralising and socialising yardstick and help create an ordered society. Is that right?
Professor	Well, to an extent… We'll look at that later, but… go on…
Student 2	Well, (against) <u>lots of schools focus on the individual.</u> Individual achievement and so on. This <u>doesn't really point towards a collective</u>… rather a more selfish belief.
Student 3	No, I think the (for) <u>socialisation is more subliminal than that.</u> Look at what school does in every country. You have to turn up on time, you have to obey the teacher. All of these things mirror what you need to do as an adult, obey rules, go to work on time, that sort of thing… pay your taxes! <ho ho>
Student 4	yes, (and social placement still goes on… which I think Parsons, Davis and Moore talked about
Professor	Yes

Student 4	Well, (for) <u>people are still ordered in school. Some go to university, some leave and get jobs.</u>
Student 1	But is this really placement? I mean does a university education place you in a more beneficial role.
Professor	Actually, there are some good statistics on that which were referred to in the lecture ...

Exercise 5
Tutorials – Not really used. Perhaps online for example: online tutorial

Seminars – Same as UK

Lectures – Same as UK

Other differences – People often refer to university as college

Exercise 6
Tutorials – Working through or discussing work. Groups of 10–20

Seminars – Not really used.

Lectures – Same as UK

Exercise 7
A lab or lab session
Usually where there is a demonstration or experiment taking place. The academic or demonstrator will show students what to do and ask questions. Students might then carry out the demonstration/experiment themselves.

Exercise 8
See individual chapters for comprehensive answers

Exercise 9
A: improve his referencing/check everything is referenced
Situation: tutorial

B: make an appointment to see Dr Dexter
Situation: Corridor/Public place – in passing

C: think about practical applications of creative development
Situation: seminar

Chapter 10

Self-evaluation
1 Chapter 4   2 Chapter 7   3 Chapter 1
4 Chapter 8   5 Chapter 2   6 Chapter 5
7 Chapter 6   8 Chapter 3   9 Chapter 9

Exercise 1
Students' own answers

Suggested answers:

Jing

3, 5, 6, 8

Albert

2, 5, 6

Susanna

1

Exercise 2
Students' own answers

Exercise 3
Students' own answers

Exercise 4
1 His father to check   2 New words
3 Everything   4 Indian, Chinese, Arabic

Exercise 5
1 Repetition of listening every day and vocab activities

2 Include some way of measuring progress like a test

3 It doesn't fit with theories of effective learning

4 Listening to complex ideas and their relationships

5 Keep a learner diary on listening to lectures and review it

Exercise 6
Student's own answers

Exercise 7
1 Number   2 Grammar   3 Word stumble
4 Losing the thread   5 Grammar
6 Losing the thread

Exercise 8

> **Key**
>
> <u>Underlined</u> = stressed word
>
> **Bold** = unstressed words
>
> _ = connected speech
>
> ~~d~~ = disappearing sound
>
> ( ) = extra sound inserted
>
> Bold and Italic = schwa /ə/
>
> / / = changing sound

1 So,(w)_one of **the** <u>key</u> (j)_aspects_of_using_ ac*t*ion research_**is** to **be** clear <u>why</u> this methodology (j) **is being**_implemented. (Key and why are stressed for emphasis)

2 **Y***ou* know, although some still believe Drummond's theory (j)_**on** teaching practice, **it's** diffic*u*l~~t~~_**to** see <u>how</u> (w)_**it** works_**in**_ modern teaching contexts. (the speaker's voice indicates scepticism).

3 Let's now turn **to**_(w)_*a*n_example_of,_**of** politics .. sorry policy (j)_~~and~~ how governm*e*nt policies_*a*ffec~~t~~_**the** curriculum. (the speaker hesitates and makes an error)

4 **We've been** mainly looking_*a*t child_education so far **this**_semester so next week **we'll be** (j) expanding **this**_**into** (w) ad*u*l~~t~~_training. (American accent)

5 What **can** we learn **from** <u>this</u>_study? (speaker uses rising intonation for a question) Well, firstly **th**at detailed feedback_**is** necessary **f***or* students_**to** progress_**in** thei~~r~~_writing. (the underlined words are stressed for emphasis)

6 Today's lec*t*ure (r) **is gonna** (r) address_ **some**_of **the** factors **th**a*t*_you (w) ough~~t~~_**to** be thinking_*a*bout **for** y*our*_research project. (fast speech)

7 Now, **this**_idea (r) of classroo~~m~~_management **can be** (j) use~~d~~_**to** (w) *a*ddress_student behaviour_**in**_**a** variety (j) **of** ways.

8 One_of **the** things we (j) **are** <u>not</u> **going to** cover_**is**_educational psychology because_ **it's**_outside **the** scope_of today'~~s~~_session.

9 **Can** you (w) all see **the** graph_**on** this slide? (pause) Okay, **in** that case let's_analyse_**it** some_more.

10 There_*are* several points_here: <u>student</u> motivation, <u>teacher</u> motivation **and the**_(j_) <u>ethos</u>_**of the** (j) institu*t*ion. (the speaker uses rising and falling intonation for a list and stress for emphasis)

Lecture 5: Learner autonomy

Preparation 1: possible answers.

Read some general websites to familiarize yourself with the topic.

Do some reading from a textbook on the topic and make some notes.

Look up some key vocabulary and write the definitions.

Discuss what you know about the topic with another student.

Preparation 2–3 Students' own answers

Authentic lecture sample answers
lecture notes:

> Lecture 5. Learning module: Learner Autonomy
>
> Anonymous, 23/02/12
>
> Slide 12: L styles
> <u>Reflect on lrn processes 2 b a better learner.</u>
> Identification of lrn styles.
>
>   H & M ————→ activist
> reflecter
> theorist
> Pragmatist etc
>
> Other labelling systs on slide.
> Find out via questionaires.
>
>   <u>Gardner</u>——→<u>Multiple intelligences</u>
>   <u>All intelligent in diff ways.</u>
>   7 ints: ~~musical, ling, spac, inter/intra~~
>   Poss more too

Slide 13: Mult intels

Interper – sensitivity to moods/feelings of others
Mus – ability to appreciate rhthm / pitch
Spac – 3D visual accuracy. Thinking in pics
Intraper – Self knowledge
Ling – Sounds rholths of words

Log/Math – recognize pattern
Bod/Kin – good physical expression

Could be a naturalist int too.

Slide 14:

Think of <u>PURPOSE</u>
       before/during/after

       This will help show benefits

Slide 15:

Lrner aut is cooperation/collaboration.
Done thru needs analysis + lrn styles
doing this   self awareness   learners
                    ↑   ↑

Lecture 5: Learning module – Learner Autonomy

Anonymous 23/02/12

Learning styles (slide 12)

In order to be a better learner <u>it</u>
<u>is important to reflect on learning</u>
<u>processes.</u>
These learning processes/styles are
usually identified via questionnaires.

Honey and Mumford identified learning
styles as: activist
                        reflector
                        theorist
                        pragmatist

This list is incomplete. Possibly
worth reading more?
Also see slide for others who
categorized learning styles.

<u>Howard Gardner</u> (slides 12 and 13)

Gardner developed the idea of
<u>multiple intelligences</u>. That people
have intelligence in different ways.

Gardner identified 7 intelligences
(and said there may be more):

Interpersonal – sensitivity to moods/
feelings of others

Musical – ability to appreciate
rhthm / pitch
Spacial – 3D visual accuracy.
Thinking in pics
Intrapersonal – Self knowledge

Linguistic – Sounds of words *(get a*
clearer explanation?)

Log/Mathematical – recognizing pattern

Bod/Kin – good physical expression

The Purpose of Learning (slide 14)

In order to see the benefits in
learning and what the learner is
doing they should focus on <u>why</u> they
are doing it (before/during/after the
activity).

Conclusion (slide 15)

Learner autonomy is about cooperation
and collaboration. This is done
through needs analysis and awareness
of learning styles. <u>These kinds of</u>
<u>activities raise self awareness,</u>
<u>which in turn makes people better</u>
<u>learners.</u>

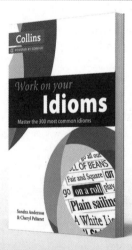